IT'S PANAMA'S CANAL !

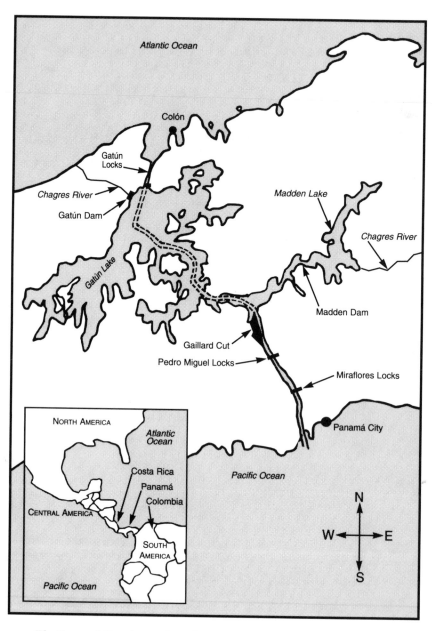

The Panamá Canal cuts through Panamá from Colón to Panamá City.

IT'S PANAMA'S CANAL !

PATRICIA MALONEY MARKUN

LINNET BOOKS
1999

First published 1999 as a Linnet Book,
an imprint of The Shoe String Press, Inc.,
2 Linsley Street, North Haven, Connecticut 06473.

Library of Congress Cataloging-in-Publication Data

Markun, Patricia Maloney.
    It's Panamá's canal! / Patricia Maloney Markun.
        p.   cm.
    Includes bibliographical references and index.
    Summary: Discusses the history and operation of the Panamá
    Canal and the events leading up to the end of American control
    at the end of 1999.
        ISBN 0-208-02499-9 (lib. bdg. : alk. paper).
        1. Panamá Canal (Panamá)—History—Juvenile literature.
    2. Panamá—Foreign relations—United States—Juvenile literature.
    3. United States—Foreign relations—Panamá—Juvenile literature.
    [1. Panama Canal (Panamá)—History. 2. United States—Foreign
    relations—Panamá. 3. Panamá—Foreign relations—United States.]
    I. Title.
    F1569.C2M155   1999
    972.87′5—dc21   99-37092
                                                              CIP

The paper in this publication meets the minimum requirements of
American National Standard for Information Sciences — Permanence
of Paper for Printed Library Materials, ANSI Z39.48-1984. ∞

Designed by Sanna Stanley

Printed in the United States of America

*T*o Sybil, Meredith, David and Paul,
who walked to school on the Orchid Path,
Wondering if the mountain lion would return,
Grew up with two languages and two cultures,
Still love them both, and the Isthmus as well.
¡Felicidades!

CONTENTS

Acknowledgments   ix

Chronology of Events   xi

1. A CONTAINER SHIP MAKES A TRANSIT   1

2. BUILDING THE PANAMA CANAL: 18
   A TIME FOR HEROES

3. HOW THE CANAL CAME TO BE   38

4. IT'S PANAMA'S CANAL!   52

5. TOWARD A SEAMLESS TRANSITION: 61
   ONE TEAM, ONE MISSION

6. "A CANAL IN GOOD CONDITION"   73

7. WHAT TO DO WITH A FIVE-BILLION-DOLLAR
   GIFT   81

8. WILL PANAMA SUCCEED IN A BIG JOB?   91

More Resources   105

Index   109

ACKNOWLEDGMENTS

The author acknowledges appreciation for information and generous assistance during the writing of this book to Panamá Canal Commission staff in Washington, D. C., and in the Republic of Panamá, in particular Cynthia Riddle, Michael A. Bragale, Mercèdes Morris García, Roxanna Cain, and Captain Orlando Allard. For political information, much thanks is due Brittmarie Janson Perez, Ph.D., Panamanian anthropologist. Robert P. Holman, M.D., Clinical Assistant Professor of Medicine at Georgetown University School of Medicine, kindly gave advice on yellow fever and malaria. B.I. Everson, former Canal Zone engineer and E-mail Canal Link correspondent, advised helpfully on engineering matters. Warm hospitality in the Panamá tradition of *mi casa es tu casa* was the gift of Elizabeth M. Dillon and her sons and daughters-in-law during my research time in Panamá.

Photographs are courtesy of The Panamá Canal Commission, unless otherwise noted.

CHRONOLOGY OF EVENTS

1502 Columbus stops on the Isthmus of Panamá.

1513 Balboa is the first European to see the Pacific Ocean.

1849 Gold is discovered in California.

1855 Panamá Railroad built across the Isthmus of Panamá.

1869 Suez Canal opens in the Middle East.

1881 French arrive to build a canal on the Isthmus.

1888 French withdraw; company disbanded in following year.

1898 Spanish-American War

1901 President McKinley assassinated; Teddy Roosevelt becomes president.

1902 Spooner Act authorizes American negotiation of a canal on the Isthmus with Colombia.

1903 Panamá revolts from Colombian rule; the United States recognizes the new Republic of Panamá on November 3. Hay-Bunau-Varilla Treaty signed designating an American canal on November 18 and giving $40 million to Bunau-Varilla's French canal company; ratified by Panamá on December 2.

1904   Americans arrive in Panamá to build the canal.

1914   Panamá Canal opens on August 15. Colonel George Goethals named first governor of the Canal Zone.

1932   Harmodio Arias Madrid elected president of Panamá; Hull-Alfaro Accords signed during his term, paving the way for changes in the Hay-Bunau-Varilla Treaty over the next forty years.

1977   Carter-Torrijos Treaty places Canal Zone under Panamá Canal Commission (P.C.C.) control. It also mandates Panamá takeover of the Canal in the year 2000.

1977– Panamá Canal Commission prepares for Panamá
1999   takeover of the Canal.

1999   December 31, 1999 at noon. It's Panamá's Canal!

A CONTAINER SHIP
MAKES A TRANSIT

IN A DRIVING RAIN AT SIX O'CLOCK IN THE
morning, Captain Nestor Castillo, a Panamá Canal pilot,
stands up in the launch that has brought him to a large ship
anchored inside the breakwater of the Panamá Canal in the
Atlantic Ocean. A sudden breeze moves the launch up and
down in choppy waters. Captain Castillo grabs a rail and
waits. On a high wave he reaches for the sturdy ropes of the
Jacob's ladder that hangs down from the deck above.

He climbs up the fifteen wooden steps of the ladder to
the deck of the *Tobias Maersk*, a container ship out of London. His assistant pilot, Captain Edgar Tejada, follows him.
Captain Castillo, with his assistant pilot, will take this ship—
528 feet long and 92.6 feet wide—through the Panamá Canal
today.

The night before, an accountant had determined from
computer records that the *Tobias Maersk* had transited the
Canal before, and its measurements had been determined.
The proper toll for a ship this size with a certain number of

Captain Nestor Castillo, Panamá Canal pilot, arrives at the bridge of the Tobias Maersk, *ready to take the container ship through the Canal. Captain Derek Golding, master of the ship, waits in the background.*

containers aboard has already been paid to the accountants by the ship's agent. There are no charge accounts at the Panamá Canal!

The schedule of transiting ships for March 17, 1999 was put together during the night and printed out on the computer for pilots to see. Captain Castillo sees by the printout that *Tobias Maersk* was given number ten, southbound. Because of the way the narrow neck of the Isthmus of Panamá lies, the Canal runs nearly north and south for its 50-mile length. For that reason, a ship heading for the Pacific Ocean is considered southbound, while a ship going the other way, to the Atlantic, is called northbound.

The *Tobias Maersk*, waiting inside the breakwater, has been notified of its place in the day's schedule. The Canal is open twenty-four hours a day, and averages thirty-eight ship transits in that time. Today just thirty-five are scheduled. A third of that number are called "Panamax ships"—jumbo vessels more than 100 feet wide and 700 feet long. Some of them are cruise ships. Others are tankers or container ships. These ships require a "clear Cut," which means that they cannot pass another ship in the narrowest part of the Canal, the Gaillard Cut. It is one-way traffic for the time it takes to move the Panamax ships through the Cut. Smaller ships wait or are scheduled to go earlier or later than the giants which need the whole Cut to maneuver in. Even though the entire Canal is well lighted, it is easier for pilots, and more interesting for cruise ship passengers and for the crew of a Navy ship, if a Panamax ship goes through during daylight. The *Tobias Maersk*, although slightly smaller, will go through Gaillard Cut with the Panamax ships today.

A ship's officer greets the pilots, and leads them to the stairs that go up to the bridge of the ship. There are twelve flights of stairs, with six steps in each one. The bridge on this vessel is very high. After climbing all the way up, the pilots are shown into the bridge, a large area with big windows and an open porch on either side to give excellent visibility to the captain. It will serve the pilots well today while Captain Castillo steers the ship through the Canal.

A member of the crew takes down the yellow and blue "Request a pilot" flag. He now raises two pennants, one for

number one, the other a zero, together making the number
10 for this transit. Above the number pennants, a half-red
and half-white flag flies, meaning, "There is a pilot aboard."
Number pennants placed below the pilot flag mean that the
ship is southbound to the Pacific, as indeed the *Tobias Maersk*
is. Number pennants above the pilot-aboard flag mean that
the ship is northbound to the Atlantic.

Captain Derek Golding, the British captain, comes forward and introduces himself. He and the pilots shake hands.
This captain has gone through the Canal many times, and he
knows well that Captain Castillo will be in command of the
Tobias Maersk during the transit.

This is the only canal in the world where the pilot assumes full responsibility for a ship during its transit. For that
reason, children who live around the Canal think of pilots as
the local heroes, especially when they see a huge passenger
ship moving safely through a lock with only a few inches of
space to spare from the walls on either side.

Captain Castillo looks out at the good view of the wall of
containers stacked up in front of him and below him on the
deck of the ship. Container ships now constitute 14 percent
of the business of the Panamá Canal. They are an essential el-
ement in international trade. The cargo on these ships is in
"containers," large metal boxes either 45 or 20 feet long.
When a ship reaches port, these containers are the right sizes
to be easily lifted by cranes and loaded on railroad cars to be
shipped to an inland destination. The *Tobias Maersk* has its
own built-in crane on deck, which saves time and possibly
damage in loading and unloading the containers.

Stealing had been a major problem in ports around the

This container ship is typical of nearly 14 percent of the Canal's traffic. The containers are stacked high on deck, on top of others that go deep into the ship's holds. The ship carries its own crane so it can unload containers in ports that lack up-to-date facilities.

world when cargo was loaded piece by piece into the cargo bays of a ship. Water damage was common as well. Cargo loaded in airtight, locked containers will arrive safely and soundly. Captain Golding points out that most of the *Tobias Maersk*'s cargo is wheat, moving from Canada to Asia.

Captain Castillo receives a radio message that his will be the next ship to go through the Gatún Locks, the first of three sets of locks the ship must pass through today. The *Tobias Maersk* has been waiting, anchored among several other ships, big and small, for word to proceed.

"Slow speed ahead," the pilot orders.

"Slow speed ahead," the officer on watch repeats. The

The artist Joseph Pennell came to Panamá in 1912 to do a series of pictures of the last heroic stages of Canal construction. This sketch of the Pedro Miguel Locks with the gates in place shows the great size of each lock. Pennell's artwork is mounted in the Administration Building.

Tobias Maersk moves through the waters of the anchorage into the Canal channel. Ahead lie the Gatún Locks.

Two mighty oceans only 45 miles apart wash the shores of this country of Panamá, which lies in the narrowest part of

Central America. A chain of mountains marches from Mexico through Central America to Colombia. In Panamá the mountains become only high hills, but these hills are still too high for a canal to run at sea level across the country. The flat desert lands of the Middle East make the level Suez Canal possible, but ships in the Panamá Canal must "climb" across high places with the help of experienced pilots and a system of locks.

Here on the Atlantic Side, a ship moves at sea level for about 6 miles into the Canal. The tide in this ocean rises only about 3 feet. On the Pacific Side, the tide can rise as high as 20 feet, but the Canal was built so that ships can move safely at high or low tide. Between the locks on the Atlantic Side and those on the Pacific Side lies the 85-foot-high level of Gatún Lake, one of the largest manmade lakes in the world, and the dangerous curves of Gaillard Cut, carved through the rock wall of the Continental Divide.

For a ship to go from one ocean to the other, it must be raised from sea level up 85 feet in three stages, about 28 feet at a time. It stays at 85 feet for most of the way across the Canal, until it takes the three steps down into the other ocean.

The raising and lowering of the water level, and therefore of ships, is done by three double sets of locks or "water stairs." A lock is a very high-walled chamber with gates at each end. On the Atlantic Side the three sets are all together at Gatún. On the Pacific Side, because of the lay of the land, one set is at Pedro Miguel, and the two remaining ones are at Miraflores.

As Captain Castillo approaches the Gatún Locks from

the Atlantic, two high metal gates, each one 65 feet wide and 7 feet thick, swing open. Here the water inside the lock is at the same level as that around the entering *Tobias Maersk*. The ship moves forward, guided by lines attached to six electric towing locomotives, three running on tracks on each side of the lock chamber. (These locomotives are called "mules." Long ago mules were used to pull ships through smaller canals. When the Panamá Canal first opened in 1914, its electric locomotives were nicknamed "mules." The name has stuck.)

Attaching these lines to a ship from the towing locomotives is a unique skill in the Canal operation. Expert line-handlers on the bow of the ship toss "messenger lines" which are used to retrieve wire cables from the locomotives. When a cable is hauled on board the *Tobias Maersk*, line-handlers hold tension on it while others slip the loop at the cable's end— called the "eye"—over the large cleat on the ship's deck. This tricky maneuver is one that has not changed since the Canal opened. Throwing the messenger line is a local skill. Competitions are held annually for champion line-throwers.

When all the lines are attached and it is time to move the ship through the lock, the two front locomotives or "mules" do the actual pulling. The middle two help control the ship by pulling or braking as the pilot commands. The last two act only as brakes. When the ship is inside, the lock operator in the control tower swings the gates closed behind it.

Now the operator turns a handle. Fresh water from Gatún Lake, moved by gravity, rushes down into huge, 18-foot culverts that run below each lock chamber, and pours into the lock through a hundred openings in its walls or floor. As the

An electric locomotive, or "mule," at the Miraflores Locks. The sign above reads in English and Spanish, "Assuring the passage into the twenty-first century."

water level rises, so does the ship, until it is at the level of the next lock ahead. The water of Gatún Lake is higher than in any of the locks before they are filled, so it takes only eight minutes for 26 million gallons of water to fill the lock chamber!

Now the operator makes the gates in front of the ship swing open, and the *Tobias Maersk* moves forward into the second chamber with the help of six electric locomotives. This chamber is at the same water level that the first chamber was after being filled. Captain Castillo watches carefully to see that the 92.6-foot-wide ship stays in the middle of the 110-foot-wide lock chamber.

The operator turns on the water, and the process is re-peated. Then it is done a third time in the final chamber. The last gates swing open; the locomotives move the ship through. The towing cables fall away from the ship. The pilot presses a button that blows the ship's whistle.

"Clear of the locks!" the whistle means. As if happy to es-cape the confining space of three locks in a row, the ship ad-vances out at 85 feet above sea level, right into the fresh waters of Gatún Lake.

This huge body of water was created, beginning in 1910, by building a mile-and-one-half-long earth dam, the largest in the world at the time, to hold back the waters of the Cha-gres River and allow the 163 square miles of Gatún Lake to cover the area. A makeshift town in its way was covered with water, and many farms had to be abandoned. Even the Panamá Railroad, the only way across the Isthmus, lay in the path of the growing lake and had to be rerouted. For several years Gatún Lake was the largest artificial lake in the world.

This is one of the most beautiful parts of the transit, as the *Tobias Maersk* passes jungle-covered islands, many with the pink, red, and yellow flowered blooms of trees in dry sea-son. Two hollowed-out log canoes called *cayucos* go by out-side the ship channel. Teams of three or four members are practicing for the annual *cayuco* race across the Canal, a three-day event held each Easter weekend. Started by Boy Scouts at Balboa High School many years ago, the race was expanded to include girls' teams, and now even Canal employees take part.

Round thatched roofs on poles, called *bohios*, peek out as shelters on some islands and peninsulas in the lake. Families

At the Gatún Locks, a container ship is moving into the first lock from the Cristóbal break-water in the Atlantic Ocean. It will go up to 85 feet above sea level in three lockages, and sail out into the fresh water of Gatún Lake to begin its journey through the Panamá Canal.

can lease these pieces of land on Gatún Lake for fishing and boating.

Now the ship is passing a big island with a high hill on it. One can hear the loud, eerie sounds of howling monkeys. That cry identifies Barro Colorado Island, the home of the Smithsonian Institution's scientific station. When Gatún Lake was created by damming the Chagres River, animals in the flooding jungle fled to high places to avoid being drowned. Barro Colorado Island was bigger and higher than

Taken from the bridge, this photograph shows passengers gathered on the bow of the cruise ship, Vision of the Sea, *which is going to "squeeze" through the lock ahead. This Panamax ship is 105 feet wide— while the lock is 110. That means the pilot will have only 2 1/2 feet of room on each side. The deck top seen here is much wider than the hull which must pass through the lock.*

most, and it soon became a naturally-made zoo. By law the Smithsonian Institution took charge of the island, and its right to remain was assured by treaty in 1978.

On Barro Colorado the animals roam free, and the scientists there live in what could be called "cages"—the reverse of the ordinary zoo. It is an excellent site for scientists to study tropical animal behavior, and they come from around the

world to do so. On another island just beyond Barro Colorado, a nature conservancy area has been created with nature trails for groups of tourists who want to observe jungle animals and birds.

While going through the lake, several ships pass heading in the opposite direction. Some are large ships which had a "clear Cut"—one-way traffic—while going through Gaillard

Cut. One is a white-and-blue cruise ship whose decks are crowded with tourists enjoying and photographing their view of the Panamá Canal. A stream of happy music floats out from the ship as it passes. Cruise ships are a growing business for the Canal.

A little later, on the port (left) side of the *Tobias Maersk* one can see the broad stream of the Chagres River coming into the Canal, as the ship passes the town of Gamboa, home of the Canal's dredging division.

After that, opposing traffic moves aside into anchorages as the ship comes to the narrow confines of Gaillard Cut with the Panamax ships. This section of the Canal has given engineers and geologists the most problems during Canal construction days and ever since. A tugboat snuggles up to the stern of the *Tobias Maersk* and follows the ship throughout the eight miles of the Cut. There is no obvious need for a tug, but in case of a loss of power or of steering in this narrow waterway, having a powerful tug right on the scene could prevent an accident.

The midday sun is very bright, and Captain Castillo pulls down the brim of his Panamanian straw hat as he looks at the first set of ranges posted on the shores to guide the pilots. These markers are black crosses painted on white signboards and placed in pairs, one above the other, in the hills. The pilot steers his ship so that the lower cross of each pair appears to be lined up exactly with the one above it. Lining up the markers in this way helps him to stay in the deep channel of the winding cut.

Captain Castillo raises his binoculars to check the ranges again.

"Starboard ten. . . . Midships. . . . to five," he commands calmly. Minute by minute these brief orders to port or starboard (right) keep the ship in the middle of the tricky channel.

A constant distraction to the pilot is the widening of the Cut that is going on along the shores. The dipper dredge *Rialto M. Christensen* works near one shore, while farther on huge trucks take turns filling up with rocks and dirt from a power shovel on land.

Now the *Tobias Maersk* is in sight of the Continental Divide. This is a stretch of high ground from which the rivers of a continent flow in opposite directions. Here the worst slides in the Canal's history have taken place. Gold Hill on the left is being shaved off, as the sounds of jackhammers around it testify. In 1974, a landslide from this hill sent a million cubic yards of dirt into the Cut. Canal traffic was closed for several hours until it was found that enough depth remained to permit one ship to proceed. Dredging began at once.

Captain Castillo relaxes as the ship moves ahead now, and the Pedro Miguel Locks come into view. With a "Beep, beep!" the tug leaves the *Tobias Maersk,* as it has made it through the Cut safely.

The gates of Pedro Miguel Locks open, and when the lockage is complete, the *Tobias Maersk* has gone down 31 feet. The ship now goes through little Miraflores Lake for one mile at 54 feet above sea level. At the two-chambered Miraflores Locks, the ship goes down 27 feet in the first lock, and another 27 feet in the second one.

In all, it took 52 million gallons of water to put the ship through six locks. All this water is lost to the oceans. The

Canal was built with locks in the belief that the eight-month rainy season and Panamá's rivers would always furnish enough water to run a lock canal.

The first severe water shortage occurred early in 1998 when the weather phenomenon called *El Niño* changed weather in many parts of the world, including Panamá. At one point in February and March only ships with a draft of no more than 36 feet could transit the Canal. Some ships simply had to lighten their loads in order to get through a shallower Canal. By June, however, the overdue rainy season began in force, and conditions were soon back to normal. Once more the guaranteed draft for ships was 39.5 feet.

As the last set of gates opens and the *Tobias Maersk* passes through, Captain Castillo calls out, "Cast off lines! Thanks and good afternoon!"

He picks up his radio and reports to Transit Central. "We are clear out of the locks. No incidents. Good afternoon."

The ship goes under the Bridge of the Americas that, in a sense, joins North and South America, and moves alongside the protective causeway that marks the Pacific entrance to the Canal. British Captain Golding and Panamanian Captain Castillo shake hands and wish each other well. After the pilot goes down the Jacob's ladder and steps into his waiting launch that is alongside the ship, he looks up and returns a wave to the bridge. High up there Captain Golding is smiling, as if in relief that the *Tobias Maersk* has made it through the Panamá Canal again without a scratch. No ship captain enjoys having someone else—even the most competent pilot— in command of his vessel.

Down come the pennants—number 10 and "There is a pilot aboard."

"Full speed ahead!" Captain Golding orders.

With a mighty blast of her whistle, the *Tobias Maersk*, guided safely from the Atlantic Ocean to the Pacific, heads for the open sea. A long journey lies ahead to deliver a hold full and a deck stacked high with containers of wheat for Singapore.

BUILDING THE PANAMA CANAL: A TIME FOR HEROES

SUCCESSFULLY CONSTRUCTING THE PANAMA Canal—"the eighth wonder of the world," it was called—was a ten-year-long job that lasted from 1904 to 1914. It involved more than 30,000 workers. A large number were American, a few were Panamanian, and some thousands were tall, muscular men largely from the islands of Jamaica and Barbados. With the fighting spirit of President Theodore Roosevelt urging them on, the "ditch diggers," as they called themselves, went into the newly marked-off Panamá Canal Zone in 1904 to dig a canal.

They were not the first. Ferdinand deLesseps, the enterprising Frenchman who had built the successful Suez Canal in Egypt, had gone bankrupt in the attempt. From 1881 to 1888, under agreement with Colombia, his company had battled lack of money, earth slides, a devastating earthquake, and death on a massive scale before they gave up. The French left their dead behind, and on silent hillsides from Atlantic to Pacific the new arrivals could see untended French cemeteries

William C. Gorgas

marked with rusty metal crosses. Most of the deaths had been from yellow fever and malaria.

WILLIAM GORGAS—FIGHTING FEVER FIRST

This was a time for heroes, and there were many, known and unknown, who worked to build the Panamá Canal. One of the first to come and the last to leave was Colonel William Crawford Gorgas of the United States Army Medical Corps. President Roosevelt had been advised by physicians at the prestigious Johns Hopkins University Medical School to send an expert in tropical diseases to Panamá.

Gorgas had recently returned from Havana, Cuba, where he had helped to clean up that city from yellow fever and malaria after the Spanish-American War. He was there when Dr. Walter Reed discovered that infected mosquitoes are carriers of yellow fever and malaria. This astounding medical information spread very slowly throughout the world. Gorgas would have a hard time convincing people that this was true. Senior members of the U.S. Congress hesitated to appropriate funds to kill mosquitoes, because they thought it a waste of money and time.

A seven-man committee had been named in Washington to be in charge of everything that was happening in the new Canal Zone. They had to approve all material orders and major decisions. Colonel Gorgas went to see them to get the disinfectants, oil and kerosene, and quantities of screening he needed to begin the battle against mosquitoes in Panamá. He also asked for a number of people to start to clean the swamps, the water cisterns, and the ditches where mosquitoes would breed.

When Colonel Gorgas got to Panamá he was assigned quarters in the old Ancon Hospital the French had built. In his building, he learned, more Frenchmen had died of yellow fever than in any place else. There were no screens on the building, and mosquitoes swarmed through it. He found malaria mosquitoes in the pans of water that the hospital beds stood in to keep ants from crawling up on the beds. Out of twenty-four Catholic nuns who had been sent there from France, two still lived and were working there, although they were suffering from recurrent malaria. The others had died of yellow fever or malaria.

A fragment of the staff Colonel Gorgas had asked for arrived—seven men, one nurse, and one physician. He asked John Wallace, who had been appointed Chief Engineer, for medical supplies and a big staff to work to rid the area of mosquitoes. But Wallace didn't believe in Gorgas's theories about how people got malaria and yellow fever.

Gorgas did not give up, though. He knew that he was right. In studying about the deaths of the 19,000 French company employees, he found that many more had died of malaria than of yellow fever. He decided that the *Anopheles*, the malaria mosquito, was the first one to fight.

With his small staff Gorgas divided Panamá City into eleven sections, and filled out cards listing the location of every well, cistern, water jar, and other open container of water in which mosquitoes were growing. Chief Engineer Wallace had chosen the old French Administration Building in Panamá City for his headquarters. Gorgas's inspectors went through the building and found mosquitoes breeding in water-filled glass containers which held brushes used in copying documents. When he tried to convince Chief Architect M.O. Johnson to have the windows of that building screened, Johnson wrote to a friend that he had little faith in modern ideas on yellow fever transmission, and he was too busy to order screens.

In the autumn of 1904, Gorgas went to Washington to try in person to get the supplies to rid the Isthmus of mosquitoes. Again he got no support. Before he left some of his friends urged him to resign, but Gorgas was not a quitter. Instead, he brought his wife back with him. They had both had yellow fever before they were married, so they were immune from the fearful disease. Gorgas was determined to convince the Canal management that he could get rid of the diseases, if they would only let him fight the mosquitoes.

Soon after he returned from his trip to the United States, the first Canal employee died of yellow fever. There were six more cases in December, eight more in January of 1905. American newspapers featured headlines, "Yellow Jack in Panamá!" In Panamá itself, the *Star and Herald* newspaper regularly published a yellow fever report with a listing of the number of new cases and the number of deaths.

In May, a yellow fever panic developed among Canal workers, and three-quarters of the American workers quit and left for home. Yellow fever broke out in the unscreened Administration Building, and M.O. Johnson, the architect, died of it. Funeral processions took place every day, and funeral trains went daily to the cemetery at Monkey Hill (renamed Mount Hope) on the Atlantic Side. While all this was going on, Chief Engineer John Wallace and his wife sailed for New York, taking with them the steel caskets they had pessimistically brought to Panamá. Wallace resigned, and was replaced by a real engineering hero, John Stevens.

GORGAS GETS HELP

Stevens was the engineer who built the Great Northern Railroad from St. Paul, Minnesota, across the mountains of the west to Tacoma, Washington. James J. Hill, the millionaire who headed the Great Northern, called Stevens the greatest construction engineer in the country. He advised President

Roosevelt to get him to head the Canal project. And Roosevelt did.

Stevens came to the Isthmus when morale was very low, and he seemed to arrive with a sense of what really was important. In one of his first speeches to Canal workers he said, "There are three diseases in Panamá—yellow fever, malaria, and cold feet. And the greatest of these is cold feet." Of course one couldn't really have cold feet in the tropics, but he meant that people were scared—of disease, of the tropics, of whether the Canal project would succeed. One of his first acts was to move the headquarters of the engineering division from the old French Administration Building on Avenida Central in Panamá City to above the muddy morass of Culébra Cut, where the most difficult excavation for the Canal would take place.

"The digging is the least thing of all," Stevens said. He ordered new towns to be built with houses, churches, schools, more hospitals, laundries, sewer systems, mess halls and clubhouses. He knew he could not keep workers for long if they had none of the comforts of home. He ordered all work stopped in Culébra Cut, and sent the steam shovel operators back to the States for the time being while towns were built and workers' needs attended to.

John Wallace, the former chief engineer, had assigned workers to live in the long abandoned, mildewed and cobweb-covered quarters the French had used. Some of the old buildings had been almost strangled by jungle in the twenty or more years since the French had left. Besides the cockroaches and snakes in this housing, workers had a special fear of the scorpion. This hideous black insect, about 6 inches long with a near-fatal stinger, hid in cracks in the wooden walls in the daytime, and came out at night. Workers were advised to inspect their shoes in the morning before putting them on, because that was a favorite hiding place of the scorpion.

Stevens and Colonel Gorgas got along well from the start. Whatever Gorgas ordered, Stevens okayed—even orders for screening for $90,000, which was a great deal of money in 1905. The doctor's small staff swelled to 4,000. They spread 50,000 gallons of kerosene a month over swamps and cesspools and any other puddle of water on the Isthmus.

In the cities of Panamá and Colón, the houses were fumigated over and over again to rid them of the dread mosquitoes—both the *Anopheles*, which carried malaria, and the *Stegomyia fasciata* (later called *Aëdes aegypti*), the carrier of yellow fever. There were nine species of mosquitoes in Panamá, but the only way to be sure that the disease carriers were being killed was to kill them all.

Even though malaria, pneumonia, dysentery, and diarrhea continued to kill more people than yellow fever, Gorgas now decided that yellow fever had to go first. It was such a fast killer, often in a few days, that people were terrified of it. If he wiped out yellow fever, he would wipe out *fear*. Malaria was slower moving, and sometimes medication helped, even though the French had lost more lives with malaria.

Gorgas found himself at the head of the most expensive and extensive health campaign in the world's history. He ordered 3,000 garbage cans, 1,000 brooms, and 500 scrub brushes, along with 120 tons of pyrethrum powder (for fumigation), and 300 tons of sulphur.

It took Gorgas a year and a half to rid the Isthmus of Panamá of yellow fever. The epidemic was over by September of 1906. Some weeks later Gorgas and some of his staff performed an autopsy on the body of a yellow-fever victim in Ancon Hospital. "Take a good look at that man," Gorgas said. "It is the last case of yellow fever you will ever see." And he was right. *Stegomyia fasciata* was gone from the Isthmus of Panamá, and so was the disease it carried to humans.

Back in Washington some of President Roosevelt's advisers were still trying to get rid of Colonel Gorgas and his new mosquito ideas. The president asked his friend and hunting companion, Dr. Alexander Lambert, what he thought. Lambert said, "You are facing one of the greatest decisions of your career. If you fall back upon the old methods of sanitation you will fail, just as the French failed. If you back up Gorgas and his ideas and let him pursue his campaign against the mosquitoes, you will get your canal."

Roosevelt took his friend's advice, and gave all support to Gorgas's efforts to clean up the Isthmus, whatever the cost. Eventually it became known as one of the most healthful tropical places in the world.

JOHN STEVENS BEGINS EXCAVATION

Chief Engineer Stevens worked eighteen hours a day while he got to know the job at hand and planned for the future. He was a railroad man, and he saw the Panamá Canal largely as a railroad project. Digging a big ditch through the Continental Divide at Culébra Cut was like moving a fantastic quantity of railroad freight. Millions of yards of dirt would have to be

Culébra Cut, now Gaillard Cut, being dug by steam shovel, January 1913.

transported someplace else—much of it to the Pacific Ocean, some to the huge earth dam at Gatún, and to any other place that needed building up. Stevens, the engineer who had built a railroad through the Rocky Mountains of North America's West, was not put off by the need to move the slippery slopes of Culébra Cut.

Stevens saw that the rickety old Panamá Railroad that the Americans had bought from the French was to be the lifeline of the Canal Zone. The French equipment, however, was too light for the tropics. On his first trip to Culébra Cut,

Stevens saw that six of the seven little, old French locomotives working there had gone off the tracks. He ordered big locomotives, such as the Great Northern Railroad used. Heavy new railroad tracks replaced the spindly rails of the French, and the distance between rails was to be five feet. The standard gauge of North American railroads was less than that: four feet, eight-and-a-half inches, to be exact. Stevens felt that it would take a broadly-based railroad car to haul away the mud of Culébra Cut.

By the end of 1906, there were 24,000 workers on the Canal project, more than the French had ever had at one time. Half of these put up the new towns promised to the workers. Others were at work improving the strength of the railroad, which was truly the backbone of the whole Canal effort. Everything moved by train—the dirt being excavated, supplies from ships docking in Colón and Cristóbal, and people traveling from ocean to ocean or even from Panamá City to Colón.

Stevens realized that the greatest challenge in building the Canal would be Culébra Cut (later named Gaillard Cut for the Corps of Engineers colonel who completed excavation there). He wrote in a letter to a Washington official of the Canal project, "Nothing but dogged determination and steady, persistent, intelligent work will ever accomplish the result. And when we speak of a hundred million yards of a single cut not nine miles in length, we are facing a proposition greater than was ever undertaken in the engineering history of the world."

By early 1906, sufficient equipment had arrived and the town-building was progressing, so Stevens could resume ex-

Two steam shovels meet in Culébra Cut in May 1913. There was great competition between steam shovel crews to see which one could excavate the most dirt in the Cut. The work was extremely discouraging because with no warning a slide could start and bury a steam shovel completely.

cavation. Steam-shovel operators were called back, and digging "a hundred million yards" of dirt out of Culébra Cut could begin again.

A SEA-LEVEL OR A LOCK CANAL?

When Stevens had first come to Panamá, he assumed that like the French plan, he would be digging a sea-level canal from ocean to ocean. That was before he observed the tremendous flood force of the Chagres River in rainy season. He changed his mind, and began to think of a lock canal with a large dam at the end of the world's biggest artificial lake to hold the water of that river.

President Roosevelt called a conference of American and European engineers with experience in canals to consider which way to go. The French in the conference kept referring to the Suez Canal as the perfect example of a sea-level canal. Suez, being in the middle of a sandy, flat desert, had no raging tropical river to deal with and no Continental Divide to dig through. However, a majority of the conference voted for the sea-level canal.

A minority report was submitted by men who had worked on the Soo Canal, which for fifty years had been the connection between Lake Superior and Lake Huron on the Great Lakes. It was the heaviest traveled canal in the world. Its annual shipping tonnage was 44 million tons in 1905, more than three times that of the Suez Canal. Even though the Soo was closed in winter by ice, this tremendous tonnage of iron ore from Minnesota's and Michigan's iron ranges passed through the Soo during the May to October ore season. There had never been a serious vessel accident, it was reported, in fifty years of heavy traffic, since the ore boats went through the locks slowly and under control.

When the U.S. Senate was voting on whether to build a sea-level or a lock canal, Stevens came out for the lock canal. That proposal won in the Senate by just three votes, 36 to 31. Had the sea-level vote won, the Panamá Canal project may well have ended in a great failure. As it was, Stevens

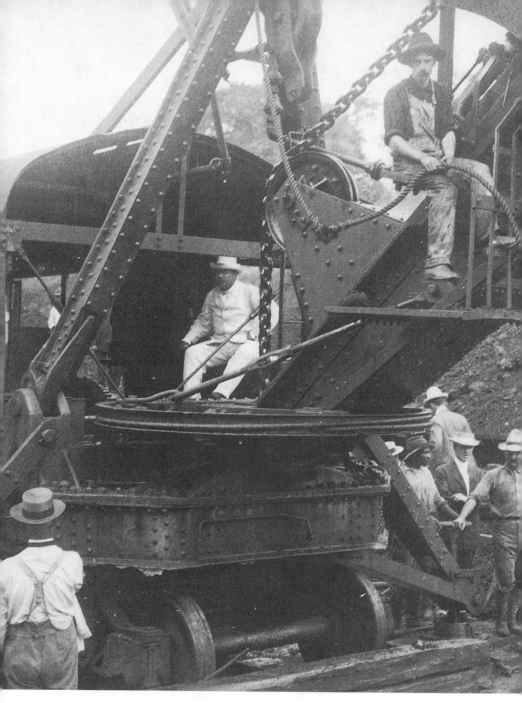

President Teddy Roosevelt at the controls, November 1906.
Courtesy of the Library of Congress

hired the chief of the Soo Canal to advise on the locks for the Panamá Canal.

TEDDY ROOSEVELT MAKES A VISIT

President Roosevelt wanted to see Panamá in the rainy season, and he went down in November 1906, the first president ever to leave the country while in office. It rained all four days he was there, but he didn't miss anything. He even jumped out of his special train and got into a 95-ton Bucyrus steam shovel at Pedro Miguel in his white suit in the rain, certainly the first American president to be photographed in such a place. He asked the shovel-runner to show him how to work the controls, and he stayed there twenty minutes playing with it. Photos of the event appeared in newspapers around the world, and Roosevelt loved it.

The Canal employees were delighted with the president's visit. In the course of construction was the Hotel Tivoli, a big, Victorian wooden structure with pillars on the front porch. When word came that Roosevelt was coming to visit, workers began hammering, sawing, and painting day and night on the hotel. They completed one wing of the structure just in time, and President Roosevelt moved off the ship and stayed at the Tivoli all four days he was in the Canal Zone, as its first guest. Throughout the Canal Zone's history, the Hotel Tivoli remained the center of parties, weddings, receptions, art exhibitions, and authors' autograph parties.

Soon after Roosevelt's visit John Stevens, worn down and exhausted from working very long days and nights, sent a resignation letter to the president. Roosevelt, who was very happy with the job Stevens was doing, was not only disappointed—he was furious.

"I'm going to get an Army man for the job," Roosevelt is supposed to have said. "He will *have to stay* until I say he can leave."

GEORGE GOETHALS—AN "ARMY MAN FOR THE JOB"

Roosevelt went to the Army Corps of Engineers and demanded their best engineer. The man chosen for the job was Colonel George W. Goethals. Some American workers grumbled when they heard that a military man was going to be their new chief. Goethals got wind of this, said nothing, but came to work wearing a white suit. He never wore a uniform in all the years he stayed in the Canal Zone. That was until 1916, two years after the Canal opened.

The new chief engineer set up meetings every Sunday morning from 7:30 A.M. until noon, when workers were free to come and air their complaints and give their suggestions. Anyone could and did come—the young and the old, workers of any color, beginners and high-salaried men. They were taken in the order that they arrived. Usually about a hundred Canal workers came each Sunday.

Goethals kept this "open forum" during his entire ten years on the job. It gave an employee the reassurance that any problem could be discussed with the man at the top. It gave Goethals a wealth of information about what was going on around him that he may not have heard otherwise. Many years afterwards he admitted that these weekly sessions gave him "control of the force."

Colonel Goethals also started the *Canal Record,* a weekly

newspaper whose purpose was to inform the employees—around 30,000 by now—about the progress being made in constructing the Canal, plus news of social events in the Canal Zone, and of the many sports workers took part in. The weekly would cover "any activities of general interest," but there was not to be any news from U.S. newspapers, and no stories praising employees. The *Canal Record* helped to create the sense of a Canal Zone community among these people who had come to Panamá from every level of American life and from other countries as well.

By 1908, Goethals was firmly in place as permanent head of the Canal project, and he made some important changes in the Canal design. Culébra Cut was widened from 200 to 300 feet. The locks were made 110 feet wide instead of 95 feet, as originally designed. The largest U.S. Navy ship, 95 feet wide, could now go through the locks, as could the largest passenger ship being built at that time, the *Titanic*. Of course that ship sank on its maiden voyage and never had a chance to transit the Canal, but most passenger ships until recently, except the *Queen Mary,* the first *Queen Elizabeth,* and the *Normandie* were built to fit through the 110-foot width of the locks. Many oil supertankers now crossing the world's oceans are too big to transit, but a pipeline has been built across the Isthmus of Panamá to transfer oil from a tanker on one coast to a waiting tanker on the other.

No matter what other part of the Canal work was going on—constructing the locks, building Gatún Dam, starting to fill Gatún Lake—the center of attraction was still Culébra Cut. Hundreds, then thousands of tourists from all over the world came by ship to see the nine-mile strip where steam

Culébra Cut, now Gaillard Cut, is blocked by yet another Cucaracha slide in 1913. In the six years that Americans had been working on the Canal, more than ten million cubic yards of dirt and rock had been removed from Cucaracha next to Gold Hill, and seven million cubic yards on the Contractor's Hill side. A dredge is working to remove the dirt that lies underwater.

shovels were filling railroad cars by the dozen. Observers who came to the site on special Panamá Railroad trains stood on hills or banks high above the scene below. The noise level was deafening. Rock drills—as many as 300 of them—made a terrible racket, while the steam shovels and the dirt trains joined in. In the distance one could always hear blasting going on.

In all, 61 million pounds of dynamite were used in building the Canal. These were more explosives than were used in any war up to that time.

Perhaps the most discouraging happenings in the whole project, for Colonel Goethals and everyone else, were the slides in the Cut. The first major one was the Cucaracha slide

George W. Goethals in his white suit (right), with President William Howard Taft on the steps of the governor's residence.

in October of 1907. Many years before, the French had had a slide at the same place. After several days of steady rain, suddenly Cucaracha started again. Rocks and dirt plunged down into the Cut, covering two steam shovels and completely blotting out the railroad tracks. For several days after that, in an area of 50 acres, part of the slope kept falling 10 to 15 feet a day. It stopped after ten days, and after a half-million yards of mud had been dumped in. In 1910 Cucaracha did it again—twice, in fact—until the south end of the Cut was bottled up for months.

As the bottom of the Cut got deeper, slides rained down more often. There were twenty-two slides in all. In 1912, more than a third of the year was spent just removing dirt after slides. Building the six sets of locks started in 1909. They were completed ahead of schedule in 1912.

The "grand opening" on August 15, 1914, was the transit of the S.S. *Ancon,* a Panamá Railroad ship loaded with proud employees, their wives, and some children, from Cristóbal to Balboa. Unfortunately, World War I had begun on August 3, and plans for world-famous people to come were cancelled. Instead the celebration was by the people who had worked on the Canal. Goethals did not board the ship, but watched the transit from beside the Canal, going by special train from one place to another across the Isthmus. One employee aboard the S.S. *Ancon* said that everything went so smoothly that a stranger looking at the ship in the locks or going through Culébra Cut would think that the Canal had been in operation for years.

Goethals, still wearing a white suit, had been named first governor of the Canal Zone early in 1914. Every governor who followed, all of them from the U.S. Army Corps of Engineers, including the last one, Major-General Harold R. Parfitt, continued Goethals's custom of wearing a white suit instead of an army uniform until the Panamá Canal Commission succeeded the Canal Zone government in 1978.

HOW THE CANAL
CAME TO BE

THE DREAM OF A WESTERN PASSAGE

IN 1502, ON HIS FOURTH VOYAGE TO THE New World, Christopher Columbus stopped in Panamá near the mouth of the Chagres River. He told the natives that he was looking for *another* ocean. They answered that, yes, there was another one not far away. If he would leave his ship, they would lead him to it through the jungle. He thanked them, and said he would go there in his ship. He sailed on and on but he never found the way to the western sea by water. There wasn't a quick one.

A few years later, some miles beyond where Columbus had landed, another explorer named Vasco Nuñez de Balboa heard the same story from the native peoples. He dared to walk inland through the jungle. From a peak in what is now Panamá's province of Darien he was the first European in the New World to see the Pacific Ocean. Panamá remembers him with a statue on Panamá City's sea wall, and the country's coinage is called the "Balboa" for the explorer.

Perhaps the first leader to express a desire to join the oceans was King Charles V of Spain, who suggested the idea of a canal across Panamá in the 1500s, but did nothing about it. Various routes across Central America's skinny spine were explored for a possible canal site in the next nearly-400 years. The Panamá route was known to be the shortest. A passage through Nicaragua which went through a lake and two rivers was one of the longest. Later, a route through the southern reaches of Mexico was favored by some as being closest to the United States.

THE CALIFORNIA GOLD RUSH

When gold was discovered in California in 1849, some adventurous people would take a ship to Colón on the Atlantic Coast of Panamá, take a boat up the Chagres River part way across the Isthmus, then get out and hike on the Las Cruces Trail, an old Spanish road, to the Pacific Coast. Once in Panamá City they would wait for the next ship going up the west coast to California. Many of them died crossing Panamá, from yellow fever, malaria, snake bite, cholera, and other causes, but enough of them made it safely across the Isthmus of Panamá to encourage American investors to build the Panamá Railroad.

This first transcontinental railroad was just 45 miles long, but it took five years to build through the jungle, with twenty-nine bridges, including a very high and long one over the wild Chagres River. An uncounted number of Irish and Chinese workers died in the building of it, and at last in 1855 a single row of tracks went from ocean to ocean. The smoky, wheezing train puffed from the new town of Colón on the Atlantic across the continent to the Pacific Ocean and Panamá City in about four hours. This first western passage began making money right away. It cost $25 in gold for a seat on the train. Many people, eager to get to the California gold fields, were happy to pay the price.

THE "PANAMA LOBBY"

American interest in building a canal across Panamá goes far back to the 1800s, and the French failure to do so. Five years after the French withdrawal in 1889, the New Panamá Canal Company (la Compagnie Nouvelle du Canal de Panamá, in French), was organized. An astute New York businessman named William Nelson Cromwell, who was general counsel for the Panamá Railroad, began looking after the affairs of the New Panamá Canal Company. From the beginning, it was clear that lobbyist Cromwell hoped to sell the defunct French company to the United States government. At this time, there was a very active group in Washington pushing for building a canal in Nicaragua.

The newspapers began talking about a "Panamá lobby" of people who wanted a canal in Panamá. The two most active men working for this were Cromwell, and a small, Napoleon-like figure, Philippe Bunau-Varilla, who had been the temporary chief engineer of the French canal project. Both Cromwell and Bunau-Varilla were big stockholders in the new company, and stood to make much money if the holdings of the old company could be sold to the United States. Bunau-Varilla, an intriguer, would become a master player in the history of the Canal. The effects of his machinations would be felt up to the present day.

Cromwell worked hard behind the political scenes to promote his company. In the election of 1900, he donated $65,000—a great deal of money in those days— to the campaign of Senator Mark Hanna in the name of the New Panamá Canal Company. For that contribution, Hanna, a powerful politician, saw to it that the Republican platform called for an "isthmian canal" and not a "Nicaraguan canal" as the Democrats had.

Incumbent Republican president William McKinley won the election, but in September of 1901 he was shot by a young anarchist and died eight days later. Forty-two-year-old Theodore Roosevelt was now President of the United States, the youngest one in the nation's history. He was an outspoken proponent of an American canal at Panamá. Roosevelt pointed out that when the Spanish-American War had started in 1898, it took sixty-seven days for the battleship *Oregon* to get from San Francisco around the horn of South America to the Caribbean for action at Cuba. It was a clear example of the need for a canal so that the nation did not have to fund a two-ocean navy.

Furthermore, the Panamá route was one-third the length of the proposed Nicaragua route, and good harbors were available on both of its oceans. There were no active volcanoes on the Isthmus, while Nicaragua had several and had no good harbors.

Congress was soon debating the Hepburn Bill, which would give the canal site to Nicaragua. A rumor arose in Washington that the New Panamá Canal Company had had a wild meeting, with much disturbance, but had ended with an agreement to sell the Panamá Railroad, several acres of land around it, two thousand buildings, and thousands of cubic yards of excavations, including much of the work done in the Culébra Cut. The price tag was $40 million. This was 60 percent lower than the original rumored price of $109 million. Even so, the Hepburn Bill—giving the canal site to Nicaragua—passed in the House of Representatives by a vote of 308 to 2.

COLOMBIA WON'T COMPROMISE

When word came to Congress that President Roosevelt really favored Panamá, Senator John Coit Spooner of Wisconsin introduced an amendment to the Hepburn Bill in the Senate. It authorized the president to pay $40 million for the New Panamá Canal Company's holdings; to acquire from Colombia perpetual control of a canal zone at least six miles wide across the Isthmus of Panamá; and to build a Panamá canal. If Colombia would not agree, the canal would be built in Nicaragua. The vote was 42 to 34. The president signed the Spooner Act two days later, June 28, 1902.

Unhappy negotiations with the Republic of Colombia for the canal treaty went on for over a year. The first Colombian delegate retired in nervous exhaustion. The second one went back to Colombia in a strait jacket after a complete breakdown. Every word, every sentence, in the first two treaties had to be checked in Bogotá. Sometimes it took three months to get an answer, and it was usually a negative one. U.S Secretary of State John Hay, a most experienced diplomat, was upset. President Theodore Roosevelt, always

*Dr. Manuel Amador Guerrero,
first president of Panamá.*

an impatient man, was beside himself. He wanted a canal
now!

The third Colombian negotiator was Dr. Tomas Herrán,
an experienced career diplomat and graduate of Georgetown
University. He spoke English perfectly. However, Colombia
was unhappy with the terms of the treaty he negotiated:
$10 million for canal rights was not enough, nor was the an-
nual payment of $250,000. Like the first two, the Hay-Herrán
treaty was rejected.

A civil war was going on in Colombia during this time,
and when some of the revolutionaries landed in Panamá,
President Roosevelt ordered out the U.S. Marines to protect
the American-controlled Panamá Railroad. This action created a furor in Bogotá, and furthered the suspicion that the
United States, which had promised Colombian sovereignty

on the Isthmus, would not keep that promise. What happened next led to the formation of a new nation—Panamá—and an unorthodox agreement which would plague the country for years to come: the Hay-Bunau-Varilla treaty.

STAGING A REVOLUTION

Dr. Manuel Amador Guerrero was one of the small group of Colombians in Panamá who were actively planning a revolution. A physician for the Panamá Railroad, Amador was sent to New York by the group to talk to William Nelson Cromwell about plans to seek Panamá's independence. He needed the support of the United States for his mission. It was through Cromwell, who wanted to distance himself from the revolution, that Amador met Philippe Bunau-Varilla.

Bunau-Varilla hinted to Amador that he had important connections in the U.S. State Department and could help, but on one condition: that the revolutionaries must entrust him to be the diplomat in Washington D.C. for the new nation of Panamá after the revolution. It was eighteen years since the wily engineer had been to Panamá, but he insisted he must be the one to draw up a canal treaty with the Americans. Dr. Amador objected. If the revolution succeeded, to have a Frenchman as its representative would be an insult to the new Panamanians. The meeting ended with no agreement on that one important item.

Within a few weeks, the revolution took place, with Bunau-Varilla using his influence to get the American gunboat *Nashville* to appear off the port of Colón at just the right time. American Panamá Railroad officials cooperated when the Colombian gunboat *Cartagena* came into Colón's harbor with 500 Colombian troops aboard. The assistant railroad superintendent, who had been in close touch with the revolutionaries for months, put together an engine and one small car and invited the *Cartagena's* officers to ride across the Isthmus in comfort. He did not tell them that he had already sent all the other railroad cars over to Panamá City, so there was no way to move the troops. The train was the only way to get to the Pacific Side.

Dr. Amador and his fellow conspirators revolted successfully in Panamá City. They bribed the head of the Colombian troops, General Estaban Huertas, by paying him $65,000 and $50 for each soldier. While the Colombian officers sat on a bench outside the barracks, a company of their soldiers marched out with fixed bayonets.

"Generals, you are my prisoners," announced the young captain in command. The officers were disarmed and marched through a crowd of several thousand people, while the crowd shouted, *"Huertas! Viva Amador! Viva El Istmo Libre!"*

Panamá raised its new red-white-and-blue flag that Dr. Amador's son, Manuel, had designed. The next morning the Colombian generals were transported back to Colón to await the next ship to Colombia. The gunboat *Cartagena* was still in Colón.

Porfirio Melendez, a woman who was friendly with the revolutionaries, took the gunboat's officer, Colonel Elisio Torres, across the street to the Astor Hotel for lunch. She told him what had happened to the generals in Panamá City and that more American help was on the way. He would be wise, she suggested, to get his troops on the *Cartagena* and leave.

When she offered him a handsome sum of money, the young colonel burst out in a fit of anger and threatened to burn Colón and kill all the Americans unless the generals were released by two o'clock in the afternoon.

Suddenly the play-acting was gone out of the revolution. All the American women and children in Colón were loaded on a German ship in the harbor and on a ship belonging to the railroad. The men went into a warehouse, and forty sailors from the *Nashville* joined them with arms. The *Nashville* steamed up, moving in closer to shore with her guns trained on the wharf and the *Cartagena*. To everyone's surprise, the *Cartagena* got up steam and left the harbor, deserting its 500 troops on the streets of Colón, where they had spent the night.

A British ship, the Royal Mail steamer *Orinoco,* agreed to take the Colombian troops back home for $8,000. They were still boarding when the American Navy's *Dixie* arrived in the harbor, and 400 Marines came ashore. The Colombian generals were released to wait in Colón for the next ship.

Cables were sent to Secretary Hay from the revolutionary leaders, then another one from the American vice-consul. The reply came that afternoon. The United States formally recognized the new Republic of Panamá.

BUNAU-VARILLA: "ENVOY EXTRAORDINARY"?

Now Dr. Amador cabled Philippe Bunau-Varilla in New York and asked for the $100,000 he had promised the group if the revolution succeeded. Amador would not, however, name Bunau-Varilla as Panamá's diplomat, and Bunau-Varilla would not send the money. Several cables went back and

Philippe Bunau-Varilla.
Courtesy of the
Library of Congress

forth between Panamá and New York. At last three of the revolutionary leaders—Federico Boyd, José Arango, and Tomas Arias—sent a cable naming Bunau-Varilla as "Envoy Extraordinary and Minister Plenipotentiary near the Government of the United States of America." Their action turned out to be a grave mistake for Panamá. Dr. Amador had an idea what Bunau-Varilla might do. He was the only one of the revolutionary committee who had met the crafty man.

The next day Philippe Bunau-Varilla and Secretary of State John Hay had lunch together in Washington. Rather disturbing to Hay was an article in the morning newspapers about a special commission just then sailing from Panamá to New York to make the Canal treaty.

Bunau-Varilla told Hay, "Mr. Secretary of State, the situation harbors the same fatal germs—perhaps even more viru-

lent ones—as those which caused at Bogotá the rejection of
the Hay-Herrán Treaty."

What a statement for Hay to hear, after spending long,
nervous months with the suspicious, uncooperative Colombians! The Frenchman went on, "So long as I am here, you
will have to deal *exclusively with me.*"

Hay was happy to hear that. After all, these new Panamanians had been Colombians until a few days ago. He did
not know that on the ship was a friendly, pro-American commission, all of whom spoke English and none of whom were
like the isolated people in far-away Bogotá. Paying their own
way, these men were coming to Washington to help their
newly independent country get a start.

The next day a cable came to Hay from the American
vice-consul Felix Ehrman in Panamá. "I am officially informed," it read, "that Bunau-Varilla is the authorized party
to make treaties."

It is a mystery who "officially informed" the vice-consul
of that. Dr. Amador, Carlos Arosemena, and Boyd, who were
on the high seas going to New York, would not have agreed.
They wanted to discuss all treaty clauses before signing.
Bunau-Varilla had been named only to make adjustments, if
needed.

A lawyer friend of Bunau-Varilla, Frank Pavey, came from
New York to meet Bunau-Varilla in Washington, and the two
of them wrote a treaty that they felt would pass in the Senate
by the needed two-thirds majority. Secretary of State Hay
worked on the treaty, too. As a model, they used the Hay-Herrán Treaty, which had been rejected by Colombia. Panamá
would get $10 million and an annual annuity of $250,000, as

Colombia had been promised earlier. Bunau-Varilla's and Cromwell's French company would get the $40 million it demanded for its railroad, buildings, machinery and unfinished digging on the Isthmus of Panamá.

The failed Hay-Herrán Treaty had specified a piece of land 6 miles wide for a canal zone. Bunau-Varilla made that 10 miles. It would cover in all 553 square miles, which would include 191 square miles of water after Gatún Lake was created. The leasehold was for 100 years and was renewable "in perpetuity." The "in perpetuity" words, *without mention of 100 years*, were then included in the Hay-Bunau-Varilla Treaty. Those two words have irritated Panamanians ever since, as has the deletion of the 100-year leasehold provision.

Bunau-Varilla arrived at Hay's home to sign the treaty on November 18, 1903. He had just had word that Amador and the other Panamanians were on the train from New York and would arrive in two hours. Hay got out an inkwell that had belonged to Abraham Lincoln, and Bunau-Varilla, representing Panamá, signed first. Then Hay added his large signature.

In two hours Philippe Bunau-Varilla was at the railroad station to meet the Panamanians' train from New York. He greeted them with these words, "The Republic of Panamá is henceforth under the protection of the United States. I have just signed the Canal Treaty."

THE FINAL BLOW: A TREATY UNDER PRESSURE

Dr. Amador, Carlos Arosemena, and Federico Boyd were shocked, then livid with rage. Federico Boyd is said to have struck Bunau-Varilla across the face. Still, the Frenchman

tried to get the Panamanians to sign the treaty before it went
to the U.S. Senate. They refused. He took them to meet Secretary Hay, thinking that the diplomat's grace and courtesy
would move them. Hay even promised a supplementary
treaty to correct any defects in the treaty just signed by
Bunau-Varilla. This promise was not carried out.

The Panamanians said they had no authority to act on
the treaty. That must be done in Panamá, and they would
take the treaty back on the ship with them. At once Bunau-
Varilla sent the whole contents of the treaty by cable secretly
to Panamá's new minister of foreign affairs, Dr. F.V. de la Espriella. He indicated that the Panamanian group had behaved
very badly, and that he wanted immediate ratification of the
treaty by cable. Minister de la Espriella replied, refusing to rat-
ify.

The Panamanians wrapped the treaty in the Panamanian
flag and put it into a small safe, surrounded by cotton. They
took it to New York and sailed for Panamá on *The City of
Washington*. After they had gone, Bunau-Varilla sent another
cable to the minister of foreign affairs. If Panamá did not rat-
ify the treaty, he threatened, the United States would withdraw its protection of the new nation of Panamá and sign a
treaty with Colombia instead.

Of course nothing of the kind was planned by the White
House or the State Department. This was Bunau-Varilla's doing. In fact, he said, "This time I hit the mark! The Government of Panamá was at last liberated from the morbid
influence of its delegation."

The following day he received cabled instructions from
Panamá—from José Arango, Tomas Arias, Manuel Espinosa,

and Minister de la Espriella—that the treaty would be signed as soon as it arrived on the Isthmus. And indeed it was, on December 2, less than a month after the revolution on November 3. And the masterful double-dealing of Bunau-Varilla wounded Panamanians deeply and for a long time to come.

IT'S PANAMA'S CANAL!

FRIENDLY RELATIONS: THE CANAL ZONE AND PANAMA

IN THE EARLY DAYS, RELATIONS BETWEEN the people of Panamá and those Americans who ran the Canal in the Canal Zone were quite peaceful. The language barrier tended to keep Americans in the Zone and Panamanians in Panamá City, except for those who had the good fortune to learn the other language, be it English or Spanish. Many American housewives made weekly trips down to Panamá City's big open air market by the sea to buy shrimp, fish, fruits, and vegetables, fresh flowers, and other items not available in Panamá Canal commissaries. On the Atlantic Side, shoppers went into the city of Colón for the same reasons. It was a good way for Americans to practice Spanish, and for the vendors in the markets to learn English.

Because of the difference in the school year calendars, the children of both cultures had a hard time getting together. Panamanian children went to school during the rainy season, May to December, and had summer vacation during dry season, January to May. Canal Zone children followed the September-to-June schedule of schools in the United States. Spanish was taught to all the children in the lower grades, and it was an elective for middle and high school students. Children did get together if American children went to Panamá for Spanish dancing and castanet lessons, and for piano, violin, and other instrumental lessons with Panamanian musicians. Canal Zone Girl Scouts met with the *Muchachas Guias*, the Panamanian Girl Scouts, and some Panamanian girls joined American troops. Boy Scouts from the Canal Zone went camping in the mountains of Panamá's Chiriqui Province, not far from the border of Costa Rica.

When roads were completed to Panamá's interior—first rough gravel roads, and at last the PanAmerican Highway built with U.S. financial assistance—it was possible to drive all through Panamá, on to Costa Rica, to Mexico and to the United States. Many Zone residents, who could not own property in the Canal Zone and had to rent government quarters, built or rented vacation homes on Panamá's many beautiful Pacific beaches or in the highlands of El Valle or Cerro Campana, both within a few hours' reach of the Zone. As roads improved, some went as far as Chiriqui Province on the Costa Rican border, and invested in coffee *fincas* (farms) or cottages in the beautiful valley of Boquete, while others favored the slopes of El Baru, an extinct volcano.

These incursions into Panamá's beautiful countryside were good ways for Americans to know Panamanians better, and to learn or practice Spanish. This helped to create a bilingual generation. As time went on, American-Panamanian marriages became common. By 1960 it was estimated that 30 percent of Canal Zone Americans were part Panamanian. Many of these people—some of whom are U.S. citizens—are staying in Panamá, and are among those trained to run the Panamá Canal.

THE MILITARY IN THE CANAL ZONE

In the ten years of Canal construction, there was little military presence in the Canal Zone, except for Colonel Goethals and a few Corps engineers and the U.S. Army Medical Corps represented by Colonel Gorgas and his staff. World War I brought more military—U.S. Army, Navy, and Marines—to protect the Canal. Permanent army bases were built at Quarry Heights, Fort Amador (named for Panamá's first president), and Fort Clayton, as well as Navy bases on both oceans.

World War II brought a great influx of all the military forces. Albrook Air Force Base and Howard Field were built by the Army Air Corps, one on each side of the Canal on the Pacific Side, and France Field on the Atlantic Side was part of the Navy installation there. The Navy was very active in submarine patrols, and defenses were set up to protect the Panamá Canal on all sides. During the war the numbers of military personnel far outnumbered the American and Panamanian Canal workers. After the war, the military did not decrease their numbers to pre-war levels. The Canal Zone was a good place for military families: There were quarters available that had been built during the war, as well as golf courses and swimming pools, movie theaters and libraries. There were also huge Army commissaries that supplied groceries at low

Fort Amador as it appears today, shows the size and complexity of the military installations in the Zone. As discussed in chapter 7, it is slated to become a tourist facility when the Canal becomes Panamá's. In the distance, the Bridge of the Americas crosses the canal.

prices for the military and for the diplomatic corps at the U.S. Embassy in Panamá.

After World War II, Albrook and Howard Air Force bases were used in transporting troops and families. Their aircraft were used for help in hundreds of emergencies in Central and South America—hurricanes, earthquakes, fires, and floods. The U.S. Air Force always arrived with food and medical supplies. As many Latin American diplomats remarked later in 1998, the Canal Zone military planes and their help were sorely missed in the bad Central American hurricanes of that year.

THE HULL-ALFARO ACCORDS

The founding fathers of the Republic of Panamá, who had dared to overthrow the remote Colombian rule at Bogotá, were all part of Panamá's upper class. Even today those names are familiar: Arango, Boyd, Arosemena, Obarrio. Members of these and other wealthy families were elected as presidents of Panamá from 1904 to 1932.

A radical change came to Panamá with the election of Harmodio Arias Madrid in 1932. From a poor Spanish-Indian family in the interior of Panamá, Arias had made his way to London to graduate from the London School of Economics, and eventually to become an attorney. He resented the presumption of the United States that it could protect independent countries from invasion or colonization by European nations. Such was the legacy of the Monroe Doctrine, which had been written one hundred years earlier, and about which Arias wrote a book. In the early part of the twentieth century, the Monroe Doctrine had been interpreted by the United States to justify American intervention in Central and South American affairs. Arias also saw the roots of many potential injustices embedded in one treaty—the Hay-Bunau-Varilla Treaty of 1903—which had given the U.S. the right to build the Panamá Canal.

As the leader of the new urban middle class in Panamá, Arias set to work to get American attention to the thirty-three-year-old treaty. Discussions with President Franklin Delano Roosevelt and Secretary of State Cordell Hull resulted in the Hull-Alfaro Accords of 1936, in which the United States renounced the right to invade Panamá to protect American interests. Also, the annual fee for the use of the Canal Zone was increased by $80,000 to $430,000. These funds came out of Panamá Canal tolls.

TREATY CONCESSIONS, 1955–1975

This was only the beginning. Nineteen years later in 1955, a Treaty of Mutual Cooperation and Understanding increased the annual payment to Panamá again, this time to $2 million per year. The treaty allowed access to increased Panamanian businesses in the Canal Zone (and fewer things sold in the old Panamá Canal commissaries). It set down a basic wage principle for all Zone employees, regardless of nationality.

Five years later it was agreed to fly the American and Panamanian flags at flagpoles of equal height outside the Administration Building in Balboa Heights, the most prominent spot in the Canal Zone. Eight years after that it was agreed that wherever an American flag flew in the Canal Zone, a Panamanian flag would also fly. This produced a flurry of new flagpoles at schools, hospitals, clubs, and other public places.

Just after school vacation over Christmas in 1964, some teenager dared to fly the U.S. flag alone at Balboa High School as a bad joke. Unfortunately a group of University of Panamá students heard about it, and decided to march on Balboa High School in protest. Before they crossed the border they ran into an angry mob who were protesting a labor dispute in Panamá. Agitators appeared, and violence was stirred up. Looting began at a row of shops on Fourth of July

Avenue, the street that divided Panamá from the Canal Zone. A fire started in which a few of the looters died of smoke inhalation. The U.S. Army sent troops to the border.

News about the riot made headlines around the world. The hotels were full of reporters and photographers from American and European newspapers and television stations who were eager to hear of any little happening to add excitement to the incident. Perhaps the most upset about the skirmish was President Lyndon B. Johnson of the United States, who was planning to run for a second term, and did not want any problems with Panamá.

In September 1965 President Johnson and President Marco Robles of Panamá signed an agreement to replace the Hay-Bunau-Varilla Treaty with another one that would give Panamá sovereignty over the Canal Zone and abolish the hated "in perpetuity" clause. If the United States wanted to build a new canal, there would have to be another treaty. For two years quiet negotiations went on, and somehow the news was leaked to the public. There was a great outcry, and President Johnson, already deeply involved in the Vietnam War, decided to postpone the negotiations.

In 1968 Richard Nixon became president, and in his one-and-a-half terms before he resigned to avoid impeachment, no treaty with Panamá was mentioned. Nor did President Gerald Ford take action during his brief term.

THE CARTER-TORRIJOS TREATY OF 1978

Early in his one-term presidency, 1976 to 1980, Jimmy Carter set about to right what he thought were some of the errors in United States' foreign policy. One was Panamá's objections to

U.S. control of the Canal Zone, which cut the little country into two parts. The United States had built the high Bridge of the Americas so that Panamanians could walk or ride over the Canal. There had always been a ferry across the Canal on the Pacific Side. The bridge that replaced it was a much faster way to go, but that did little to improve the discontent in Panamá.

The Hay-Bunau-Varilla Treaty of 1903 in which no Panamanian had input continued to cause unrest among Panamanians. Now, seventy-four years later, President Carter proposed a treaty to give the Canal Zone, and ultimately the Panamá Canal itself, to Panamá. Panamanian president Omar Torrijos went to Washington, and the Carter-Torrijos Treaty was drawn up. Once approved by the U.S. Senate and the Legislative Assembly of Panamá, it would give immediate possession of most of the lands and towns in the 10-mile-wide zone around the Canal to Panamá, with the exception of the Panamá Canal itself and some military bases.

A period of twenty-two years was provided for, during which Panamanians would be trained in the skills necessary to run the old and complicated waterway. At noon on December 31, 1999, Panamá would take possession of the Canal and all other lands.

At the insistence of Congress, another treaty was prepared, to which Panamá grudgingly agreed—a neutrality treaty which gave the United States the right to intervene in Panamá should peaceful transits be jeopardized or hostile acts be committed in the Canal. In a vote of the Panamanian people, 64 percent of the citizens agreed to both treaties.

In the U.S. Senate, a tremendous battle raged over

Carter's plan to give the Canal and the Canal Zone to Panamá. Panamá employed a lobbying firm to change American public opinion to support the treaties. Retired Panamá Canal employees who were active in the Panamá Canal Association in every state wrote letters to their senators pleading with them to vote against the treaties. Hundreds of them had spent their whole working careers in the Canal Zone, and they could not agree that abolishing the Canal Zone was the solution to the problem of the Panamá Canal. After a long, slow journey through the Senate, the treaties were approved—by just one last-minute vote of one senator.

The Panamá Canal was, according to the treaties, placed under the control of the new Panamá Canal Commission (PCC). This organization of Panamanians and U.S. citizens has worked well for the past twenty-two years to educate the people of Panamá in the skills needed to run the Canal.

TOWARD A SEAMLESS TRANSITION: ONE TEAM, ONE MISSION

A "SEAMLESS TRANSITION": HOW TO MOVE from American management of the Panamá Canal to Panamanian control without a difference in the operating efficiency of this waterway, so long respected around the world. That was the aim of the Panamá Canal Commission when it took over the running of the Canal from the Panamá Canal Company and the Canal Zone government six months after the treaty signings and approvals in 1978.

THE PANAMA CANAL COMMISSION

The Commission was a nine-member group, made up of five Americans and four Panamanians. Its mission was to prepare a small country to manage and maintain one of the busiest and most important canals in the world. Governing the former Canal Zone went from American courts and Canal Zone police to Panamanian control. Throughout the treaty period, four of the nine members on the Commission's board of directors have been Panamanian. For the first ten years a Pana-

manian served as deputy administrator. Since then the Canal
has had a Panamanian administrator.

Since August of 1996, Señor Alberto Aleman Zubieta has
held that job. On December 31, 1999, when Panamá assumes
full control of the Canal, Señor Aleman will become the Chief
Executive Officer of the Panamá Canal Authority (PCA), the
Panamanian company that will take the place of the Panamá
Canal Commission. Four of the current members of the Commission's board of directors will be members of the PCA. The
"seamless transition" will be complete. To establish the PCA,
Panamá had to pass an amendment to its Constitution, as so
much of Panamanian life will be affected by the ownership of
the Canal.

One basic change mentioned in the amendment is that
the Panamá Canal will be run for profit. Toll rates set in
1914 by the United States were raised only twice—in 1974
and 1976—before the new treaties were signed in 1978.
Since then they have been raised five times, most recently in
1998.

A NEW WORK FORCE FOR THE CANAL

When the treaties first took effect, there were 5,521 Panamanians and 2,105 American workers for the Panamá
Canal. Twenty years later, in late 1998, 70 percent of all professional and managerial jobs were held by Panamanians,
and 95 percent of the skilled-craftsman jobs. On the Canal
itself, over 82 percent of the floating equipment operators—
of barges, tugs, dredges, and so forth—were Panamanian.
Now 72 percent of all Panamá Canal pilots are also Panamanian.

The apprentice program has made it possible for many Panamanians to learn new skills or improve those they already have to qualify for jobs with the Panamá Canal in the next century.

Starting in 1985, Panamanian college graduates have been encouraged to enter the Canal's career intern program. This gives special training for jobs such as computer programmer; for electrical, mechanical, and other kinds of engineers; for marine traffic controller; accountant; and other professional positions.

The apprentice program recruits craftsmen for Canal operations. All 140 current apprentices are Panamanians. Another program called Upward Mobility trains employees for hard-to-fill positions, and gives men and women in "dead

Canal jobs are often performed near very deep water, and workers such as this man must wear life vests for safety.

end" jobs a chance to move ahead. There are forty-four Panamanians in this program.

At first the Commission posted signs at the University of Panamá and advertised in Panamanian newspapers about the opportunities for jobs at the Panamá Canal. Knowledge of English was no longer needed for most positions, although English is the official language of the Canal until December 31, 1999. English is the language commonly used internationally at sea, as it is also the language used in international aviation. There are many jobs around the Canal that do not require a knowledge of English.

TRAINING CANAL PILOTS

One of the hardest jobs to fill has always been that of Panamá Canal pilot. Only a Class One pilot is qualified to take over from the captain of a giant cruise ship, a heavily loaded oil tanker, or a huge, highly loaded container ship like the *Tobias Maersk* in chapter 1—and to take such a vessel through the Canal.

To begin with, to be a pilot candidate one must be a graduate of a maritime academy with at least two years of licensed experience as a third officer on the high seas in charge of a watch aboard vessels of more than 1600 gross tons. Or the candidate must have experience equivalent to that, as determined by a marine bureau review board. The applicant must be able to communicate in the English language, have no physical impairments, and must know how to swim. It will take eight years, first as a pilot-in-training, then as a limited pilot of ships up to 225 feet long, and after many transits, as a pilot of ships up to 526 feet long. Once qualified, there are still seven steps to go to be at Step 8, a Class One pilot ready to take a ship of the largest size through the waterway.

Only four Panamanians were pilots when the transition period began. Qualified pilots were so scarce for a time that Class One pilots who had gone to live in the U.S. were flown back to Panamá at company expense for several weeks' work at a time.

Training more Panamanians to qualify for existing positions of towboat master and of pilot became a priority, and the Panamá Canal Apprentice School set in motion suitable maritime training programs. In 1983 these programs were consolidated and revamped. It has been found that on-the-job training coupled with a thorough understanding of the Canal operation and knowledge of the area are the most effective ways to accomplish training goals.

In 1994, a marine simulator for training and research was installed, complete with radar, to enhance the hands-on part of the training program. All the equipment an officer would find on the bridge of a ship is there for the student to use. Exercises conducted in the simulator include approaches to locks, dockings and undockings, anchorings and maneuvering in various situations involving multiple traffic, ships or dredges, during simulated day or night time, in clear or foul weather. The pilot trainees are exposed to emergency situations that may occur any time during a typical transit: the vessel's engine may fail; the steering system may give way; or there may be a fire aboard. How the student reacts as he sits in command on the simulator going through what seems to be the Panamá Canal is reviewed, and, if needed, advice is given on the correct response.

A pilot has been described as *someone who has to know almost everything without consulting anything*. When a pilot is in the middle of a blinding tropical rainstorm in the Canal, it is not the time to look up the compass course for the next reach. It's not the moment to check the depth of the water outside the channel or to look up the number of the buoy where the ship is supposed to make the next turn. These are things the Panamá Canal pilot must know even better than his own name.

A Panamax vessel—the largest class of ships to go through the Panamá Canal—could be described as a large, slow dynamic system. It is the largest object which is deliberately designed for motion that is constructed by man. Into the holds of just one Panamax vessel could be stored the equivalent in weight of more than 250 Boeing 747s, the largest commercial airliners ever built.

A single container ship can carry so many containers that it would require a train over 20 miles long to transport them from the dock to their final destination. That ship can be more than 3 football fields long and tower 15 stories from wheelhouse to keel. These huge vessels make their way through the Panamá Canal every day.

That is a lot of metal to move around. Yet this tremendous mass is controlled by one person, the pilot. His decisions determine how safe this transit through the Canal will be. Just landing a little hard on the center wall between the locks could put a dent in the ship's hull that would cost hundreds of thousands of dollars to repair. Land extremely hard, and the pilot could cause a hole in the ship that would make it sink. These are the kinds of responsibilities that are vested in a pilot—both lives and property. That is why the pilots have always commanded so much respect.

Up until this time the Panamá Canal has always assumed responsibility for the safe navigation of transiting vessels. It remains to be seen what happens to the pilots' safety

Midshipmen of the Panamá Nautical School. Many of these young people can look forward to possible careers with the Canal.

records when the ship owners must assume the first million dollars' expense in any accident in the Canal after December 31, 1999, at noon.

The ship *Atlas,* which was built in 1934 to serve as a crane boat, has now become a training vessel. The crane was removed, and the big old *Atlas* provides six weeks of training for a variety of cadets and shipmates. They learn everything from chipping paint and painting to handling the lines during maneuvers.

Panamá Canal pilot Vic Faulkner, with twenty-five years of experience navigating the waterway, knows all the ins and outs of Canal waters. "We practice things that allow the pilots each to build a bag of tricks of knowledge. That gives them a choice of backup systems under the changing conditions they will meet as pilots," he said.

The pilot understudies (PUPs) and the pilots-in-training (PITs) spend at least thirty days training on the *Atlas* before earning their first license to pilot ships up to 225 feet in length through the waterway. They practice anchoring, docking, night-time navigation, lockages, and emergency procedures. After all their training on the simulator, now—along with all the chipping and painting—the students are learning more about what life on shipboard is really like.

Captain George A. Markham, Chief of Maritime Training, writes in the *Panamá Canal Training Manual:* "Nobody is born with the skill necessary to guide these floating leviathans through the tortuous waters of the Panamá Canal. Everyone must be trained for this job. That is the purpose of the Pilot Training Program and this book, to prepare you for that day when you will command one of these ships from one ocean to the other."

A CANAL FOR THE PEOPLE

Another part of the Panamá Canal Commission's mission has been to introduce citizens of Panamá to their Canal. Even though Panamanians have seen the Canal from a distance or crossed the Bridge of the Americas, not many except for government officials had ever had a tour of the locks. Few had ever heard a staff guide lecture in Spanish about how the Canal works. This has been done almost on a daily basis for many years for cruise passengers and tour groups visiting from all over the world.

In the time of transition, invitations were issued to clubs

Children visiting at Miraflores are introduced to the filtration plant, which processes drinking water from the Chagres River for 55 percent of Panamá's population.

and groups and to schools throughout the country, from the Guaymi Indians in the hills of Chiriqui to the San Blas Indians living on a thousand small islands near the Colombian border. These citizens are being encouraged to come and get to know their Canal. Schoolchildren are particularly welcome, because they will be the future owners of the Panamá Canal. Schools all over the Republic of Panamá are urged to introduce students to how the Canal works. During 1998, a record 52,000 students visited the Canal.

Many of the new Canal employees' families had never

"Child of the Canal Day" gave these youngsters a chance to climb up on a Panamá Canal "mule."

been to the waterway. In 1998, for the first time, the Commission sponsored a "Child of the Canal Day." All employees' children were invited to visit the Canal facility where their mother or father worked, so they could see what their parents did all day, and also to learn about the function of the Panamá Canal.

It turned out to be a real celebration, one which will

probably be held again in 1999. Some groups toured the locks. Others went to the water filtration plant to see where the drinking water that is piped to Panamá City is purified. That water from the Chagres River is provided to the majority of the population of the country.

Still other children visited the Administration Building with their parents to see the Canal headquarters. The youngsters were able to meet some of the officials of the Panamá Canal Commission as well as to see the inside of the building, which has murals on the walls showing the construction days of the Canal. Every child left his parent's work site with a better idea of what the parent's job is and more knowledge of the Panamá Canal and how it works. Next year they may learn even more.

"A CANAL IN GOOD CONDITION"

BY TREATY THE UNITED STATES IS BOUND TO turn over the Panamá Canal to Panamá in good condition. In line with that, in 1997 the Panamá Canal Commission's board of directors asked the U.S. Army Corps of Engineers to examine the Canal infrastructure and its equipment thoroughly. This study concluded that the Canal is generally in good condition, especially for its age.

However, the Engineers found more than 830 items which needed repair, and work went ahead at once to correct them. For example, the tracks and track beds of some of the electric locomotives at the locks had deteriorated in eighty-four years and needed replacing. A crane lowered new track into place where needed, after a new track bed had been prepared. Some of the lock gates were not closing correctly and had to be repaired.

In the history of the Canal, every four years the engineering division had spent two to three months cleaning the locks. Under the Commission, the locks had not been cleaned for

Gold Hill, the highest point at the Continental Divide in the Isthmus, has long been a trouble spot in the Canal. Current efforts to widen the channel are being made here, and the area still to be excavated can be seen at the water line.

eighteen years until the decision was made to clean them during June of 1998, that month being the time of lightest traffic in the Canal. Shippers were advised that traffic would be moving more slowly at that time. One lock of a pair was closed down and cleaned while traffic went through the other one.

MODERNIZING THE CANAL

At the same time, the Corps of Engineers reviewed and approved of the Commission's five-to-seven year program to modernize and widen the Canal at a cost of one billion dollars under the leadership of Panamá Canal Commission Administrator Alberto Aleman Zubieta. Although the Canal now

Repairs advised by the Army Corps of Engineers will put the rails and roadbeds of tow tracks into superior working order.

has enough capacity to handle current traffic and that of the next few years, the Commission wanted to make sure that the Canal can provide the same quality of service in the next century as ships continue to get larger.

Much of the money will be spent on the part of the Canal that has always given engineers the most problems— the area that in construction times was called Culébra Cut.

Culébra is the Spanish word for snake. In spite of its new name, Gaillard Cut, this section of the Canal snakes along for 8 miles, slicing through the Continental Divide. It was carved through rock and shale for most of the distance. Here the principal Canal excavation took place, beginning in the years of the French canal. Philippe Bunau-Varilla, later co-author of the Hay-Bunau-Varilla Treaty, started his career as a young engineer managing excavation at Culébra under the French.

A big container ship moves through the Gaillard Cut while a dredge with floating pipes attached sends its mud and rocks off for disposal. A large piece of the Cut is being chewed off here, making this channel wide enough for two-way traffic.

Here, too, the devastating and disheartening slides have taken place all during the Canal's history. The Cut was originally only 300 feet wide. During the 1930s and 1940s, it was widened to 500 feet in a "passing section" for large ships. Between 1950 and 1971, the remaining portions of the Cut were widened to 500 feet. Perhaps that seemed wide enough at the time, but the number of Panamax vessels—the largest that will fit in the Canal locks—is fast increasing. In 1996, for example, 4,125—or 31 percent—of transiting ocean-going

Two ways of digging: A new hydraulic excavator, with a fifty-ton class offroad truck ready to receive a bucketful of dirt and rocks, digs from land; in the water a dredge works the old-fashioned way.

vessels were ships 100 feet wide. Because of Gaillard Cut's narrow width and sharp turns, large vessels going in opposite directions cannot meet and pass safely in this section of the Canal. Where the Cut demands one-way traffic, ships going the other direction must wait for the big one to go through first. When possible, a Panamax ship leads the way in the morning, and also, when possible, huge ships go through in daylight, especially in Gaillard Cut.

NEW EQUIPMENT TO SPEED UP TRANSITS

The Canal has set a standard for itself that no ship should spend more than twenty-four hours in Canal waters before transiting. If one-way traffic in Gaillard Cut can be eliminated by widening the channel, the great effort will be worth it. With the help of a new, land-based rotary drill rig, the drillboat *Thor,* and the 15-cubic-yard dipper dredge *Rialto M. Christensen,* dredging personnel began to remove more than 14 million cubic yards of underwater material in 1998.

Because of recent increases in Canal traffic, especially in wide-beam vessels, the Commission decided to speed up the Cut widening, with the hope of completing it in 2002, well ahead of schedule. Additional dredging equipment was bought in 1996 and 1997, and the drilling and blasting capabilities increased.

New equipment includes a land-based hydraulic excavator with support from four 50-ton class off-road trucks. These arrived in August of 1997, and they are busy widening the Cut from the land side, rather than from underwater. This has never been done before in the Panamá Canal. The objective now is to increase channel width to 630 feet in the straight sections and 730 feet at those snake-like curves.

Other improvements include the purchase of seventeen new tugboats, seven to increase the current fleet and ten replacements for a total of twenty-four tugs in service rather than the current seventeen. At this time there are eighty-two electric locomotives, or "mules," at the locks to pull the ships through. When the new, improved models arrive, the fleet will consist of 108 locomotives.

The locks have always been controlled by a simple mechanical system devised before the Canal opened. Plans are now made to replace the system that has opened and closed the locks millions of times with a new hydraulic system.

Also in the works is a new traffic management system using satellite communications, electronic mapping, and other technologies that will allow Canal schedulers to pinpoint the location of transiting ships, working tugs, and dredges, to provide more efficient scheduling operations.

All these programs should be completed by the year 2005 and will result in a Canal capacity increase of more than 20 percent. These improvements are being funded through the current toll base.

WHAT TO DO WITH A
FIVE-BILLION-DOLLAR GIFT

THE INTEROCEANIC REGION AUTHORITY, known as ARI, was created by the government of Panamá in 1993 to "administer and promote investment in the Panamá Canal area." Much of the area has already been turned over to Panamá, and the last pieces will be in Panamá's hands before December 31, 1999. The region stretches from the Atlantic to the Pacific Ocean along both sides of the Panamá Canal. It covers more than 800,000 acres, or 2 percent of the total area of the Republic of Panamá.

Within this region there are thousands of buildings and installations, including ports, airports, hospitals, houses, schools, warehouses and power plants. In all, the land and properties are thought to be worth five billion dollars. What to do with all this property, particularly in the tropical high humidity where special care must be given buildings that mildew quickly and machinery that can rust overnight, is a tremendous job now facing the country of Panamá.

THE ARI COURTS FOREIGN INVESTMENT

The ARI—called *Autoridad de la Region Interoceanica* in Spanish—is under the direction of Nicolas Ardito Barletta, a former president of Panamá. An eleven-member board of directors appointed by President Ernesto Perez Balladares for a term of five years receives no salary. These are honorary appointments. The board decides on policies, programs, and the operation budget. It also approves contracts and concessions.

The general administrator is responsible for the business end and the legal representation of ARI. He has a staff of well-trained professionals to take care of daily business. Soon after Señor Barletta was appointed, he went on an international tour and hand-delivered to businessmen around the world a brochure describing the five-billion-dollars' worth of land and properties, to encourage interest in foreign investment.

Panamá is a small country of fewer than three million people and must depend on the work and business experience of foreigners to make use of the great number of properties and the wealth of land under its control now, or after 2000. ARI has already made a list of what it hopes to accomplish for Panamá with these investment opportunities. First, in this country with a high unemployment rate, the wealth should be used as a way of generating more jobs for Panamanians.

A North American firm, a subsidiary of the Kansas City Southern Railroad, has started to build a new railroad—the Panamá Canal Railway—on the site of the old Panamá Railroad across the Isthmus. In March of 1999, new tracks were being laid. The railroad's reconstruction is expected to take eighteen months to finish. The company hopes to transship 1,500 to 2,000 containers a day from the many container ships that come to the Canal, thus saving ships the cost of transiting the canal. It also plans to offer Panamá City-to-Colón passenger service. This will improve local mobility, as the only trans-Isthmian highway is very heavily traveled. The railroad will need to hire employees to run it, which will mean jobs for Panamanians.

THE EXPORT BUSINESS

Second, with ports on both oceans and unique access to the Panamá Canal, the country hopes to promote the export business. Already there are large areas on the Atlantic Side called "free zones," where foreign countries can store manufactured goods and then transship them to other countries as sales take place. With all this land and storage space, as well as immediate access to the Panamá Canal, the export business could become a huge Panamanian enterprise.

Evergreen, a Taiwanese shipping company, has completed the first stages of construction of the 60-acre Colón Container Terminal near the Colón free trade zone. The project has cost nearly $100 million and will soon employ 200 Panamanians. Evergreen is the largest shipping and transport company in the world. It plans to build hotels, facilities for fuel storage and fuel sales, and even a maritime school in Panamá.

Panamá's third objective is to develop new commercial, industrial, and tourism opportunities for the country. Some countries Señor Barletta contacted on his international tour have already begun investing in these kinds of projects.

When the Arraijan-Rodman fuel storage complex reverted to Panamá, Mobil Oil won the bid to assume management of the facility. This complex includes thirty-one fuel storage tanks and has access to the Rodman deepwater dock at the Pacific entrance to the Canal. Mobil will pay Panamá $25 million in the next three years for this complex. It will also pay $40,000 a year to Panamá as well as a percentage of each barrel of oil sold.

NEW TOURIST FACILITIES AND SERVICES

To attract tourists, a U.S.-Korean consortium has signed an agreement with ARI to build a $300 million resort complex on the beautiful site of Fort Amador just outside the Pacific entrance to the Panamá Canal. The site includes a popular swimming beach and a causeway 2 1/2 miles long which was built from rocks and soil excavated from Gaillard Cut. The causeway reaches out to join Flamenco Island, a high hill on which a lighthouse stands. A hotel for tourists is being built, and plans include a monorail on the causeway, a shopping center, convention hall, and eventually timeshare condominiums.

Also being considered for the Fort Amador site is a cruise ship port where passengers could disembark and enjoy a day in Panamá. In 1998, 313 cruise ships transited the Canal, and the number is growing every year. If cruise lines were to schedule a stop at such a port, there is a golf course at Amador that could be used, a swimming beach, tennis courts, and restaurant facilities at the former Amador Officers' Club.

Tourism is already Panamá's third most important source of foreign earnings after Canal tolls and international banking. The country has a great abundance of bird, animal, and plant life found almost nowhere else. It has 2,000 miles of coastline on two oceans, superb deep-sea fishing, and almost untouched waters with ideal waves for surfing. The newly acquired military bases provide buildings and recreational facilities that could be used by tourists.

The Panamá Canal itself is very popular with tourists, those aboard transiting vessels and others who visit Miraflores Locks with tour groups. The job for Panamá is to convince tourist agencies and cruise ship companies to schedule tourists to get off the ships and spend time in Panamá. Several cruise lines that feature Panamá Canal tours spend a day going through the Canal, then move quickly on to Costa Rica without even allowing tourists to get off in Panamá. The toll at the Panamá Canal is the only money the country currently takes in from cruise ships with hundreds of passengers.

If passengers could disembark, those with a few days could take tours to the San Blas Islands where the San Blas Indians have a most interesting culture; to Chiriqui, site of the beautiful valley and town of Boquete; or on the other side of El Baru, the extinct volcano, to look for birds and wildlife in the highlands along the back road to Costa Rica. Panamá has more quetzals than does Guatemala, which calls the quetzal its national bird, and more than 900 species of other birds, many of them rare. It also has twelve varieties of hummingbirds.

Panamá has been slow to develop Spanish/English guides and tour companies, but the business is now beginning. The country might do well to imitate its neighbor, Costa Rica. That enterprising land has given tour-guide training to hundreds of men and women who escort in friendly fashion thousands of U.S. tourists each year, making that country one of the most popular for these Americans to visit.

HUNDREDS OF HOMES TO SELL

A huge job for this country is how to sell the homes that formerly belonged to the Panamá Canal Company and to the U.S. military. Some of the Panamá Canal homes have been sold, but most of them have been rented since 1979. Employees of the Panamá Canal Commission who will be working for the Panamá Canal Authority after December 31, 1999, will be given the first opportunity to buy these homes, as they would be closest to their work places. Prices of the homes are now being determined.

The 468 homes on the former Albrook Air Force Base are very much wanted by Panamanians who live in Panamá City, because those homes are right next to the city. Two of President Balladares's high officials were given the former commanding general's home and a ranking officer's home to rent, with the understanding that they would be eligible to buy them. However, the ARI made a ruling that all renters will have to leave those Air Force homes before they are put up for sale. This was a well-publicized example of not showing favoritism to politicians in power. If a fair price can be set on each house and prospective buyers apply for a particular house or houses, perhaps the sale of those thousands of homes will be done honestly.

If the ARI can move on this by the year 2000, Panamanian buyers will be very happy. Some of these houses have been empty for three or four years. In the tropics buildings de-

The town of Balboa is typical of several towns in the former Canal Zone. The Interoceanic Region Authority, or ARI, is selling these homes as part of its charge to promote investment in the Panamá Canal area. In the foreground is the monument to George Goethals, more than anyone else the father of the Canal.

teriorate very quickly without regular care, and there has been no maintenance done on them.

ARMY BASE TURNOVERS

In February of 1999, the U.S. Armed Forces announced the dates of the final base turnovers:

- On June 30, Fort Sherman went to Panamá with barracks for 300 persons, a cement plant, a gasoline station, a chapel, gymnasium, and a theater that seats 200, various swimming pools, and a community club that holds 160 persons.
- On September 1, Panamá would get the buildings

and campus of the former Canal Zone College, which could certainly add fine facilities to the University of Panamá or any other college or big school in Panamá City.

- On November 1, a very large turnover would come, with Howard Air Force Base, Fort Kobbe, and Farfan, all on the other side of the Canal from Panamá City. These include 706 housing units, nine barracks, and a theater that seats 1,189 people. Also there is a school with thirty-one classrooms. An airport with runways long enough to support international flights, a passenger terminal, and the facilities for providing fuel for airplanes are waiting at Howard Air Force Base.

- On November 30, the old Army base, Fort Clayton, with many fine homes, swimming pool, golf course, library, movie theater, and chapel would be turned over to Panamá.

- The last one to go, on December 22, would be Corozal, which has a large Army commissary. There is also a mental hospital and a veterinarian's offices. The cemetery at Corozal, in which Americans for three generations have been buried, will remain by agreement the property of the United States.

ARI is responsible for a most important project to help save the watershed of the Chagres River, which supplies much of the water for the Panamá Canal and drinking water for the

The hospital complex named for Colonel Gorgas, who drove yellow fever and malaria from the Isthmus of Panamá, now awaits scientists, physicians, and other personnel to put it to good use under Panamanian authority.

majority of the country's residents. It has begun a program to reforest 8,650 acres of that land. It is now offering twenty- to-forty year concessions to businesses interested in planting and harvesting tropical hardwood trees. In twenty years, a plantation of 125 acres will produce a quantity of wood that would be valued at approximately $3.2 million. As the trees grow they will serve as shade to protect the watershed.

Many opportunities are awaiting foreigners willing to put their time and money into investing in a part of the $5 billion shower that has fallen on Panamá. Facilities such as the schools; the concrete plant; the big theaters; the college campus; Gorgas Hospital with many operating rooms, a large obstetrics and gynecology building, laboratories, and all the facilities of a modern hospital complex; and the international airport with its passenger terminal and a gasoline facility are standing silent, just waiting to be used.

WILL PANAMA SUCCEED
IN A BIG JOB?

SHIP OWNERS, TRAVELERS, SHIPPERS IN THE
international trade, and everyone else who is interested in
the Panamá Canal wonders how this country, with a population of 2,800,000—less than cities such as Philadelphia,
Houston, or San Diego—can possibly keep the complicated
Panamá Canal running for the ships of the world.

Its success depends on three groups of Panamanians:
those who run the Canal; those who govern the country; and
the will of the people of Panamá to do what is necessary to
preserve the Canal.

The Panamá Canal Commission has worked very hard
to train staff in every aspect of running the Canal, from pilot
to admeasurer (the person who measures each new ship to
figure the amount of its toll); from electrical engineer to locks
personnel. The staff of about six thousand are in place, ready
for the smooth transition. They know their jobs. They are
eager to continue to do them.

A NEW PRESIDENT, A NEW AGENDA

A most encouraging sign for the future of Panamá was the election on May 2, 1999 of Mireya Moscoso, to the presidency of Panamá. She won a good majority of votes and takes office on September 1, 1999. She defeated Martin Torrijos, son of the late military strongman Torrijos, who had helped depose Moscoso's late husband Arnulfo Arias from the presidency and went on to sign the 1978 Canal treaties. The fifty-two-year-old Moscoso, a coffee company owner, will be Panamá's first woman president. She narrowly lost the election four years ago to Ernesto Perez Balladares. By law, he cannot run for a second term, although he tried to change the Constitution to make it possible. Further, in June 1999, his PRD party passed a law through the Assembly excusing the outgoing president from attending the new president's inauguration—a slap at Señora Moscoso.

During the campaign Moscoso promised to keep politics or corruption from undermining administration of the Canal, and to protect the water basin needed to operate the Canal lock system. She repeated these promises in her acceptance speech after winning. She also said that workers and ship companies would be involved in decisions about the waterway.

Moscoso has a strong reputation for honesty and for working for the poor and underprivileged. She may have a lot of opposition to her ideas of how to run the Canal, as the PCA and the ARI are filled with friends of former president Balladares. His political party also has the majority in the Panamanian Assembly.

BALLADARES AND THE
"JEWEL OF THE NATIONAL PATRIMONY"

The Panamanian government has the power to make or break the future of the Canal. As a presidential candidate in 1994, Ernesto Perez Balladares found that voters worried about his political party's connections to the former president, General Manuel Noriega, who is currently serving a term in a Florida prison on drug charges. Balladares had been Noriega's presidential campaign manager.

As part of his own election campaign, Balladares promised that he would treat the Panamá Canal not as the spoils of victory, but "as the jewel of the national patrimony." Three years later, when it came time to name the members of the ARI, the group that decides what to do with Panamá's recent inheritance of $5 billion worth of land and properties, Balladares seemed to have forgotten about taking care of the jewel.

Of the eleven people named to the ARI, four are close relatives of Balladares or his wife. Hiring relatives for jobs in one's own organization is called *nepotism*. It is illegal in most public jobs in the United States. It is common in the governments of Latin America, where families are very close. Cousins are frequently one's best and only friends. Very often these relatives do not have the experience to do the jobs they are hired for. Balladares's relatives on the ARI, for example, know nothing about handling real estate or selling power plants. One is a first cousin, one a son-in-law, and two are the spouses of other cousins.

Although Balladares knew that there would be another

presidential election before his term expired on August 31, 1999, he went ahead to name the members of the Panamá Canal Authority, which will replace the Panamá Canal Commission on December 31. Mireya Moscoso assumes office on September 1 to a PCA that is already filled with Balladares's old political buddies—some for a term as long as nine years. None of them belongs to her political party.

An exception is the chairman, Alberto Aleman Zubieta, who moved from his post as Panamá Canal Commission Administrator since August 1996, to his current job as the first administrator of the PCA, for a seven-year term. The U.S. government passed special legislation allowing Aleman Zubieta to accept an appointment from the Panamanian government while serving in a U.S. government agency. He was educated as an engineer in the United States, and he chaired the Blue Ribbon Committee of the Corps of Engineers which made the "good condition" report on the Canal and decided on the billion-dollar Canal improvements.

Former president Balladares also appointed to the board of directors two members of his political party who had served in the cabinet of the imprisoned drug czar, General Noriega. Jorgé Ritter, foreign minister under Noriega, was appointed chairman of the PCA board of directors and boss of the experienced engineer, Zubieta. Ritter knows neither engineering nor transportation. His ties from the past raise a critical question: Is or was Ritter involved somehow in Panamá's drug business, here right next door to drug-ridden Colombia? And what could that mean for the Canal?

"This sends the wrong signal to everyone who uses the Canal and wonders if Panamá can run it as efficiently and as honestly as the Americans," said a European shipping company executive at a congress on the future of the Canal soon after the appointments. If some of those responsible for the Canal become involved in illegal business, it could prove disastrous.

THE CANAL—NOT THE ONLY ROUTE

Panamá's decision not to be responsible for the first million dollars of damage in a ship accident may convince ship owners to take out insurance during a Canal transit. This will increase the cost of transit in the Panamá Canal. If Panamá continues to raise tolls to make a great profit, international ship owners may seek alternative routes from the Atlantic to the Pacific, and vice-versa. In international shipping from parts of Asia, as well as from Australia and New Zealand, ships can take the Suez Canal if the Panamá Canal becomes too expensive. New ships are moving faster than ever. For some large, new freight ships it may be cheaper to go around South America than pay a very steep price to cross at Panamá.

Another alternative for container ships coming across the Pacific is to unload their hundreds of containers in ports such as Seattle or in Oakland, California, onto freight trains going across the United States to an East Coast port such as New York City, Baltimore, or Norfolk, and then to another ship. Overland freight may prove less expensive than greatly increased tolls at the Panamá Canal, plus insurance on the ship.

SOME SHAKY BEGINNINGS— ENVIRONMENTAL CONSEQUENCES

Little Panamá was not prepared for the first tremendous gifts of lands, of tropical rain forest, of hundreds of homes, or of the coast-to-coast railroad that it received within a few months of the treaty signing. The Panamanians had never run a railroad, and the people assigned to the job did it poorly. The railroad was not in the best shape when Panamá got it, and it rusted out in six months.

The tropical rain forest in the Canal Zone, which in part protects the 1,289 square miles of the Panamá Canal's watershed, went to Panamá. This rain forest had always been well patrolled to prevent anyone from cutting down a tree. Except for a small Boy Scout camp, there was no building in "the finest rain forest in Central America," the pride of the Canal Zone.

After it went to Panamá, a rich owner of cattle herds in distant Chiriqui somehow got permission to build a road right through the rain forest, cutting down great mahogany and tropical cedar trees. He began raising cattle there, 200 miles closer to the markets of Panamá City than his Chiriqui ranches.

Once there was a road, 200,000 landless people, many of them from the Choco tribe in Darien, moved in as squatters. They would pick out a piece of land, burn the trees to clear it, build a hut to live in and plant corn, bananas, and possibly oto or papaya. Burning helps to destroy the nutrition in the soil, and after a few crops a family would move on to squat on another piece of land, leaving a treeless open space where soil erosion would begin.

Much of the rain forest was destroyed before a Panamanian environmental group called ANCON pointed out that the water level of the Canal could go down because of the harm done to the Chagres River watershed. Seventy percent of the rain forest has already been destroyed, much of it around Madden Lake, the headwaters of the Chagres River, held back by Madden Dam. Some of the area has now been declared a national park, but signs along the road advertise new tract developments.

"They need permission to build in this protected area, but they don't get it," said Jorgé Tovar, a biologist with ANCON.

Madden Lake is becoming polluted as raw sewage is pumped into it from the thousands of homes and shacks which have sprung up around it. The sewage and a great deal of silt from so many building projects are getting into the Chagres River, which until 1978 was one of the purest rivers in the world. If Panamá does not stop growth at Madden Lake, more than half the population of the country, which now gets its drinking water from the Chagres and the filtration plant at Miraflores, will have to seek a new water source.

TOO MUCH SILT EQUALS NO CANAL

The silt problem is even more dangerous to the future of the Canal than the sewage flowing by. Soil erosion is increasing with all the construction going on around the lake and the Chagres River itself, much of it being done illegally. Sediments build up when barren land devoid of forests is rained on. As sediment levels rise, the storage capacity of these bodies of water falls, and that means a shallower draft for the Panamá Canal. In addition, soil erosion brings a great amount of nutrients into the lake. This has started to spur greater growth of vegetation, which can suck up valuable water supplies and reduce storage capacity even further.

A silted-up canal would not provide the carefully watched guarantee of water deep enough to provide a draft of 39.5 feet for ships. With more larger ships becoming Canal customers, it is essential to keep the deep draft the Panamá Canal has always provided, except for two months during *El Niño* in 1998.

Now the Panamá Canal Commission is giving programs in all the schools in the Madden Lake area. Young people under the direction of environmentalist José Tuñon are learning the importance of improving the Chagres River's watershed.

Panamá recently designated one-third of the watershed zone as national protected land. Panamá Canal employees in the future should be alert to see that no more housing is built in that national park area. To protect their jobs, they want to protect the Chagres River watershed. Panamá's incoming president Mireya Moscoso has already added her voice to those of Panamanian environmentalists.

A silted-up canal, too shallow for ships to use, may be in this country's future, says Panamanian ecologist Stanley Heckadon Moreno. In the Canal Basin around Madden Lake and behind Madden Dam, which he considers "the most critical area for the country," the annual deforestation rate is about 10,000 acres a year. At this rate Heckadon predicts that unless strong measures are taken, Madden Lake will be completely silted up and useless for water storage or to provide water for the Canal by the year 2040.

Environmental policing is necessary, but more than that must be done. The Panamanians who work at the job of running the Canal must speak out about the pollution and the silting. They must work to elect officials who will stop the de-

José Tuñon, an environmental specialist for the Panamá Canal Commission, shows a map of the watershed of the Chagres River to children of that area. Great efforts are being made to teach young people new respect for the rain forest and the Chagres River, for the Canal depends on careful stewardship. The Spanish words above the map translate: "The Canal is yours! Take care of it!"

velopment of the Madden Lake region, the cutting down of trees in the watershed, and the growth of the cattle industry there. If they teach their fellow Panamanians what is happening to the Canal watershed, the drinking water supply of more than half of the country, and the Canal they are inheriting "in good condition," they can still save it all.

BRIGHT OUTLOOKS FOR PANAMA'S FUTURE

One trend in Panamá's favor is a growth of democracy throughout Central America. Following the example of de-

mocratic Costa Rica, "the Switzerland of Central America," which has no military force, neighboring countries have abandoned the tradition of military-controlled elections. This is also true of Panamá, where three candidates competed openly in the May 1999 presidential elections.

Panamá is growing in population and in wealth. One

A large tanker, having successfully negotiated the Panamá Canal, glides under the Bridge of the Americas and heads into the Pacific Ocean.

great advantage is that the country enjoys having the dollar as its currency, an arrangement the United States agreed to when Panamá became independent of Colombia and Canal construction began. As a result of this, Panamá is now home to more than 150 international banks. It is the most prosperous country in Central America and much of South America.

Panamá City has grown at a great rate since the treaties were signed in 1978. At that time there were very few tall buildings in the city. Now they are springing up all over town. Traffic has become a major problem in the city, one of the blights that goes along with progress. Panamá has built an elevated toll road as a shortcut to the new downtown.

In Panamá's favor is progress and constant improvement in its public schools. Driving through the country on the PanAmerican Highway one sees school buses, a rather new phenomenon. Children used to walk to school or wait for a public bus along the highway. Twenty years ago the Guaymi Indian children hardly ever went to school. Now in Chiriqui and Veraguas many of these children are having the opportunity to learn to read and write.

The PanAmerican highway was being improved in the 1999 dry season, January to May, with roads being redesigned to correct dangerous curves. Pedestrian bridges for people to cross that busy highway in every town and tiny village from Panamá City to Davíd, about 150 miles away, were erected in those months. New hotels and motels have been built , not only in Panamá City, but in the city of David in Chiriqui, as well as in Boquete, Cerro Punta, and Volcán in the mountains to the east. Panamá's oceanfront property is fast becoming more valuable throughout the country.

Panamá has indeed become more prosperous. Along with this should go more honest government and less nepotism. If the government will keep the Canal out of politics and allow it to function on the well-trained skills of its employees and the leadership of its new, conscientious President Moscoso, and if the people who live in the watershed of the

Chagres River will save the rain forest and end slash-and-burn agriculture, little Panamá, like another Switzerland, should run the business of the Panamá Canal smoothly and profitably in the twenty-first century.

MORE RESOURCES ABOUT PANAMA AND THE PANAMA CANAL

BOOKS

Buckley, Kevin. *Panama: The Whole Story*. New York: Simon and Schuster, 1991. The "just cause" invasion of Panamá and the capture and subsequent conviction on drug charges of then-president Manuel Noriega.

Falcoff, Mark. *Panama's Canal. What Happens When the United States Gives a Small Country What It Wants*. Washington, D.C.: AEI Press, 1998. Contains the full text of the two treaties between the United States and Panamá, the first giving the Canal to Panamá on December 31, 1999, and the second concerning the permanent neutrality and operation of the Canal. Includes a thorough political history of Panamá.

Griffin, Adele. *Rainy Season*. Boston: Houghton Mifflin, 1996. A novel about students at Balboa High School, centerpoint of the 1964 riots on the Isthmus of Panamá.

McCullough, David. *The Path Between the Seas: The Creation of the Panama Canal, 1870–1914*. New York: Simon and Schuster, 1972. Tells the early history of the Canal and the thorough inside story of the Hay-Bunau-Varilla

Treaty, which greatly influenced the Carter-Torrijos treaties of 1978 and eventual U.S. surrender of the Canal.

St. George, Judith. *Panama Canal, Gateway to the World.* New York: G.P. Putnam's Sons, 1989. A thorough, fascinating history of the construction of the Panamá Canal. Striking photographs of appropriate historical events light up the text.

Department of Geography Staff. *Panama in Pictures.* (Visual Geography set). Minneapolis: Lerner Publications, 1987. Not only excellent photographs and maps fill this book, but informative chapters on the land, history, the people, and the economy of Panamá.

VIDEOS

Panama. Covers the construction and history of the Panamá Canal. Interspersed with rare footage from the early 1900s. ½ or ¾ inch video. Dist. by King Features Educational Division, 235 E. 45th St., New York, N.Y. 10017.

The Panama Canal. Second edition. Traces the history of the Panamá Canal from its construction to the 1978 treaties. Explains how the Canal operates and its significance to world transportation. 11 min. Dist. by Coronet/MTI Film and Video, c/o Simon and Schuster Film and Videos, 108 Wilmar Drive, Deerfield, IL 60015.

Panama Canal. Depicts ships from the Pacific entering the Canal and being lifted 85 feet by the Miraflores and Pedro Miguel Locks to Gaillard Cut and Gatún Locks. The vessels are returned to sea level by the three giant locks at Gatún. 17 min. ½ or ¾ inch video. Dist. by MCFI Productions. Hoe Mar/Chuck Film Industries. P.O. Box 61, Mount Prospect, IL 60056.

Panama Canal 1983. This program covers the construction and history of the Panamá Canal. VHS or Beta, ¾ inch. Produced by WGBH, Boston. Dist. by Hearst Entertainment/King Features, 235 E. 45th St., New York, N.Y. 10017.

WORLD WIDE WEB

Web users know that the best way to find sites concerning Panama is by using search engines such as Yahoo at <www.Yahoo.com> to find current listings of web sites. Users should always be aware that web sites can become obsolete, updating can be erratic, and site content can change.

The Panamá Canal website is www.pancanal.com.

INDEX

Pages with illustrations are in boldface.

Administration Building, 21, 23, 72

Aëdes. See *Stegomyia fasciata*

Aleman Zubieta, Alberto, 62, 74, 94

Amador Guerrero, Manuel, **43**, 44–46, 48–49

Amador, Manuel, 45

ANCON (environmental group), 96–97

Ancon, S.S. (ship), 37

Anopheles mosquito, 21, 24

Arango, José, 47, 50

ARI (Interoceanic Region Authority), 81–90, 92–93

Arias Madrid, Harmodio, xii, 56–57

Arias, Tomás, 47, 50

Arosemena, Carlos, 48–49

Atlas (training vessel), 68–69

Balboa High School, 10, 57

Balboa (town), 37, **87**

Balboa, Vasco Nuñez de, xi, 38–39

Balladares, Ernesto Perez, 69, 86, 92–95

Barletta, Nicolas Ardito, 82, 83

Barro Colorado Island, 11–13

Birds, 85

Boyd, Federico, 47–49

Bridge of the Americas, 16, 59, 60, **100–01**

Bunau-Varilla, Philippe, xii, 40–41, 44, 46, **47**–51, 76

California Gold Rush, xi, 39–40

Canal Record, 32–33

Canal visitors, 69–72

Canal Zone College, 87–88

Cartagena (gunboat), 44–46

Carter, Jimmy, 58–60

Carter-Torrijos treaties, xii, 59

Castillo, Nestor, 1, **2**–17

Chagres River, 10, 14, 29, 38, 39, 72, 88–89, 96–98, 103

Charles V (King of Spain), 38

"Child of the Canal Day," 71

Chiriqui, 53, 70, 85, 96, 102

Colombia, xi, 7, 18, 42–43, 48–49, 50

Columbus, Christopher, xi, 38

Container ships, 1, 4–**5**, 67

Continental Divide, 7, 15, 25–26, 29, 74, 76

Costa Rica, 53, 85, 100

Cromwell, William Nelson, 40–41, 44

Cruise ships, 12, 14, 84–85

Cucaracha. *See* Slides in the Canal

Culébra Cut, 23, **26–28**, 29, 33, **34–35**, 36–37, 42, 75–76. *See also* Gaillard Cut.

Deforestation, 96–99

de la Espriella, Dr. E.V., 50, 51

deLesseps, Ferdinand, 18

"Ditch diggers", 18

Drinking water, 70, 72, 98–99

Ehrman, Felix, 48

El Baru, 53, 85

El Niño, 16

Electric locomotives ("mules"), 8, **9**, **71**, 79

Environmental concerns, 95–97

Evergreen Shipping Co., 83

Ford, Gerald, 58

Forts, **55**. *See* U.S. military bases

"Free zones," 83

French railroad equipment, 26–27

Gaillard Cut, 3, 7, 13–15, 27–28, 75, **76–77**, 78–79. *See also* Culébra Cut.

Gatún Lake, 7, 8–9, 10, 11

Goethals, George, xii, 32–33, 35–**36**, 37, 54, 87

Gorgas Hospital, **89**, 90

Gorgas, William Crawford, **19**–22, 24–25, 54

Guaymi Indians, 70, 102

Hay-Bunau-Varilla Treaty, xi, xii, 44, 46–51, 56, 58, 59, 76

Hay-Herrán Treaty, 43, 48, 49

Hay, John, 42, 46–50

Hepburn, Bill, 41–42

Herrán, Tomás, 43

Hotel Tivoli, 31

Hull, Cordell, 56

Hull-Alfaro Accords, xii, 56–57

"In perpetuity" clause, 49, 58

Interoceanic Region Authority. *See* ARI

Johnson, Lyndon B., 58

Johnson, M.O., 21, 22

Locks of the Canal, **6**–9, 7–10,

11, 12–13, 15, 16, 33, 74, 79–80, 85

Madden Lake, 97–98
Malaria, 19–22, 24–25, 39
Markham, George A., 69
McKinley, William, 41
Modernizing the Canal, 74–78
Monroe Doctrine, 56
Moreno, Stanley Heckadon, 98
Moscoso, Mireya, 92, 98, 102
"Mules." *See* Electric locomotives.

Nashville (gunboat), 44, 46
Nepotism, 93
New Canal equipment, 79–80
New Panama Canal Company, 40–42
Nicaragua route, 39, 40–42
Nixon, Richard M., 58
Noriega, Manuel, 93–94

"Panamá lobby", 40–41
Panamá Nautical School, 68
Panamá Railroad, 26–28, 35, 37, 39, 40, 42, 43, 44–46
Panamá Canal Appentice Program, 63, 66
Panamá Canal Authority (PCA), 62, 86, 92, 94
Panamá Canal Commission (PCC), xii, 60, 61, 62, 69, 72, 73, 75, 91, 94, 98

Panamá Canal pilots, 1–17, 62, 65–69
Panamá Canal Railway (1999), 82–83
Panamanian Revolution, 44–46
Panamax ships, 3, 67, 77–78
PanAmerican Highway, 53, 102
Parfitt, Harold R., 37

Rain forest problem, 96–97
Reed, Walter, 20
Reforestation, 89
Rialto M. Christensen (dredge), 15, 79
Ritter, Jorge, 94–95
Roosevelt, Franklin Delano, 56
Roosevelt, Theodore, xi, 19–20, 22–23, 25, **30**–32, 41–44

San Blas Indians, 70, 85
Sea level canal, 28–29
Silt problem, 97–99
Slides in the Canal, 15, 35–37
Soo Canal, 29, 31
Spanish-American War, xi, 20, 41
Spooner Act, xi, 42
Stegomyia fasciata mosquito, 24, 25
Stevens, John, 22–28, 29, 31–32
Suez Canal, xi, 7, 18, 29, 95

Tolls, 1–2, 62, 95

Torrijos, Omar, 59, 92

Tourism, 84–86

Treaty concessions
(1955–1975), 57, 58

Treaty of Mutual Cooperation
and Understanding, 57

U.S. Army Corps of Engineers,
32, 37, 54, 73–74, 94

U.S. Congress (Senate and
House), 29, 41, 42, 50, 59–60

U.S. military bases, 54–56, 84,
86, 87–88

U.S. State Department, 44, 50

Upward Mobility Program, 63

Wallace, John, 21, 22, 23

Yellow fever, 19–22, 24–25, 39